APPRECIATING THE ACCLAIMED

Contemporary Perspectives on the Works of Sahitya Akademi Winners

Edited by

Dr. K. Anuratha

Dr. A. S. Mohanagiri

About the Editors

Dr. K. Anuradha is an Associate Professor in the Department of English at Government Arts College, Coimbatore, with more than two decades of experience as an academician. She is a distinguished scholar with a profound interest in Indian Writing in English and American Literature. Her academic portfolio is enriched by a Ph.D., signifying her deep commitment to literary studies. Dr. Anuradha's scholarly pursuits have led her to explore various dimensions of drama and literature, making her an ideal editor for the anthology "Appreciating the Acclaimed: Contemporary Perspectives on the Works of Sahitya Akademi Winners."

Dr. A. S. Mohanagiri, Associate Professor of English at Government Arts College, Coimbatore, is a distinguished academician with a Ph.D. in English. Specializing in English Language Teaching, Dr. Mohanagiri has a deep interest in Indian Writing in English and New Literatures. His extensive research and academic work, including significant contributions in the fields of literature and language teaching, make him a valuable editor for the anthology "Appreciating the Acclaimed: Contemporary Perspectives on the Works of Sahitya Akademi Winners."

CONTENTS

Examining British Exploitation in India: A Post-Colonial Analysis of Shashi Tharoor's "An Era of Darkness: The British Empire in India"

Mrs. K. Anupama

Assistant Prof. in English,
Hindusthan Institute of Technology, Coimbatore

Mrs. M. Sumithasree

Assistant Prof. in English,
Hindusthan College of Engineering & Technology, Coimbatore

Shashi Tharoor, born on March 9, 1956, is a multifaceted individual, having served as an international civil servant, diplomat, bureaucrat, and politician. Representing Thiruvananthapuram, Kerala, he has been a Member of Parliament since 2009. Tharoor's diverse career is complemented by his role as a public intellectual and writer, with a focus on post-colonial and post-modern perspectives.

Among his notable literary contributions are works such as "The Great Indian Novel" (1989), "Show Business" (1992), "India: From Midnight to the Millennium" (1997), "Riot" (2001), "Bookless in Baghdad" (2005), "An Era of Darkness: The British Empire in India" (2016), "India Shastra: Reflections on the Nation in our Time" (2015), and "Why I am A Hindu" (2018).

Through his non-fiction writings, Tharoor engages in a critical exploration of colonialism and Orientalism, presenting arguments from the perspective of the colonized. Despite the departure of colonizers, Tharoor highlights the enduring impact of suffering that lingers in the aftermath of colonization.

In May 2015, Tharoor addressed the exploitation and financial degradation inflicted by the British at Oxford University. Despite India being plundered, he advocated for more than just compensation – a fundamental acknowledgment of the wrongs committed and a sincere apology. In the initial eight chapters of his work, Tharoor compellingly illustrates how Indians, through the years up to 1751, bore the costs of their own oppression. He exposes the British government's misleading tactics that led to the colonization of India for two centuries. Tharoor's book, "An Era of Darkness," stands as a courageous act of debate, shedding light on the British exploitation. The repercussions of this exploitation persist, with India still grappling with the lingering pain inflicted by the British. That colonial era remains a dark chapter in Indian history marked by riots, famine, racism, and unprecedented economic exploitation.

Within the pages of "An Era of Darkness," Tharoor expands upon the content of his Oxford Union speech, weaving a comprehensive narrative by gathering information from various accounts. Across eight chapters, he articulates his sentiments, openly opposing the British exploitation that subjected Indians to plundering. Tharoor contends that the actions of the British were solely driven by their self-interest, providing a critical perspective on the motives behind their deeds.

He makes statements that go against what history books usually say. He gathers strong evidence from reliable sources and holds the Westerners responsible for things that didn't benefit India. He successfully created divisions in the country. Additionally, the Battle of Plassey turned out to be advantageous for Clive and officials of the

East India Company. Even though India contributed men, participated in wars, and more, the Britishers didn't pay anything to India. Tharoor argues that he couldn't find anything positive about the entire period of British rule in India. Many historians expressed anger about how their rule caused decay and was indescribable. During this time, India faced significant challenges and hardships.

"They displaced nawabsand Maharajas for a priceemptied their treasures and took over their states through various methods(including, from the 1840s, the cynical "doctrine of lapse" whenever a ruler died without an heir), andstrippedfarmers of their ownership of the lands they had tilled for generations"(Tharoor 3).

Tharoor explains how the British led to the downfall of the Indian economy. In 1700, India accounted for 27% of the world economy, surpassing all of Europe's economies. However, when the British left India, the economic situation had drastically declined, reaching nearly 3%. The author attributes this decline to the fact that India was governed primarily for the benefit of Britain. "The reason was simple: India was governed for the benefit of Britain" (Tharoor 4)

The goods produced by Indians were directly sold to Britain. Although India was a major producer of cotton, most of it was sent to Britain. Consequently, Indian weavers reduced their production, leading master weavers to become impoverished. Dhaka, now the capital of Bangladesh, was once a hub for Muslin production. However, the output plummeted from lakhs in 1760 to 50,000 by the 1820s. The widespread rural poverty was a consequence of British rule, as modern machinery rendered handmade textiles obsolete, making Indian weavers victims of technological obsolescence.

India, renowned for its steel, textiles, and ships, was reduced to a colony that produced raw materials under British rule. Upon the departure of the British, the contribution to exporting manufacturing goods dwindled from twenty-seven percent to a mere two percent. Handloom clothes, once extensively exported worldwide, saw a decline after the East India Company took over. The British displayed cruelty by mutilating Indian weavers, imposing tariffs and duties as high as seventy to eighty percent. This resulted in Indian manufactured clothes being expensive and unable to compete with British-manufactured goods, leading to the destitution of master weavers in India.

The traumatization of British rule didn't take rest. Theft in the name of taxation began and they loot millions each year between 1765and 1815. It became the favourite activity for the Britishers,and they started treating us as cash cows. Among two third of the population who were colonized by Britishers fled their lands in the late eighteenth century.

Racial discrimination was nearly legal under the British rule. Tharoor likewise says, *"Justice, in British India, was farfrom blind: it washighly attentive to the skin colour of the defendant. The death of an Indian at British hands was always an accident, and that of a Briton because of an Indian's actions always a capital crime"* (Tharoor 106-7).

Tharoor skillfully portrays the coexistence of Indians under British rule, showcasing a rich diversity in social behavior and a more flexible caste structure. There were no rigid distinctions between Hindus, Sikhs, and Jains in various regions of the nation. Across different areas, Hindus and Muslims shared common customs in terms of eating habits, marriage, festival celebrations, and religious observances. The British faced challenges in attempting to divide them. However, the introduction of census-taking in India by the British government allowed them to comprehend caste and religious disparities and their proportions within the overall population. Tharoor notes that caste and racial tensions were less harmful before the British arrived. The British, particularly in the later eighteenth century, exploited this by implementing a divide-and-rule policy based on caste distinctions revealed through the Indian census. This technique evolved over time, leading to the division of Hindus and Muslims based on their respective religions. Tharoor also points out that the British not only heightened tensions between Hindus and Muslims but also fueled disputes within the Muslim population, particularly between the Shia and Sunni philosophies.

Shashi Tharoor dismisses the notion that the British ruled wisely and benevolently for the welfare of Indians. He contradicts this perspective of "enlightened tyranny" by examining various famines, asserting that over three crore people in India needlessly perished from malnutrition during the Raj. Tharoor draws attention to studies by Nobel Prize winner Amartya Sen, who demonstrated that famines are preventable, primarily caused by a lack of access to food rather than a shortage of grain production. Tharoor highlights the paradox that, while Indians were suffering from famines, Londoners were consuming Indian food. In his book, he utilizes the account of Lieutenant Colonel Ronald Osborne, a firsthand witness, to vividly illustrate the dire conditions faced by the peasants:

"Scores of corpses were tumbled into old wells because the deaths were too numerous for the miserable relatives to perform the usual funeral rites. Mothers sold their children for a single scanty meal. Husbands flung their wives into ponds, to escape the torment of seeing the perish by the lingering agonies of hunger" (Tharoor 183-4)

The author also highlights forced migration, emphasizing that people were compelled to travel abroad on British ships. Additionally, the author mentions the existence of communal schools operated by village communities in India before the British arrival, which were widespread across the country. These communal schools faced destruction by the East India Company through force and resources, with little effort made to rebuild them. The traditional Indian education system, known as the guru-shishya Parampara, suffered significant harm due to British education policies.

Tharoor, a proud native of India, points out that five of the best educational institutions existed between the seventh and twelfth centuries CE: Vikramashila, Nalanda, Somapura Mahavihara, Odantapuri, and Jaggadala. Furthermore, he believes that the British occupation played a crucial role in the loss of oral teaching, a practice deeply revered in Indian culture. Additionally, the British ceased teaching religious and mythological writings such as the Mahabharata and Ramayana, two immortal Indian epics that could have fulfilled a similar role in Indian classrooms as the Iliad and Odyssey did in British ones. Therefore, according to Tharoor, the British bear the responsibility for Independent India's inability to continue the tradition of teaching secular classics.

A nation boasting a rich culture, material wealth, an educational system, and diversity is recounted as a tale marked by broken geography, unsettled people, and suffering. Through the Rear-View Mirror, a reflective tool reminding the British of their past atrocities, Shashi Tharoor meticulously unfolds this narrative with the support of data. The present-day Indians did not exist during the colonial era; they once aspired to live in a free environment. The term "Dark Ages" refers to a historical period when colonial control was ruthless, and Indians paid the price with their time, money, generosity, and blood.

Tharoor's "An Era of Darkness" originated as an eight-chapter discourse at Oxford when a notable Indian speaker filed a lawsuit seeking reparations from Britain and India. Rather than requesting a substantial amount of money or a percentage of the British economy, Tharoor insisted on a pound and a public apology for the next two hundred years. He believed that the apology would be immensely beneficial. The video of this Indian on British soil, employed by one of the world's most renowned firms, went viral, serving as a reminder to the British of their actions and why they shouldn't take pride in them.

The Indian penal empire imposed rules such as the cut press, treason, and Article 377, all of which continue to impact the nation today. Tharoor pointed out that in response to protests against the ruling party, 58 Indians were detained on treason and homosexuality accusations in just two years. Tharoor, a member of the Indian National Congress, acknowledged criticism in his famous Oxford speech, stating, "The party that has misled India for six decades has always been insulated with pride, corruption, just like its British rivals," as shared by Jonathan Foreman.

Tharoor acknowledged the validity of the criticism and stated, "History cannot be reduced to a game that contrasts the errors of various time periods. Every age must be broken down into its individual accomplishments and disappointments." This book refers to a time when we inhabited our own soil, consumed our own food, and inhaled air that nourished our lungs. However, their age makes them resemble prisoners held in the Plato Cave, where their legs and necks were fixed, and nothing but shadows appeared on the wall nearby. Yet, their eyes lack light where we live. The shadows are realistic for them. If we stand outside that cave today, after being freed in India, and gaze at the sun, feeling its warmth, perhaps now is a good moment to revisit that cave, see what that time was like, and draw lessons from it.

The book successfully draws the reader into its pages. The author claims that the great history of colonial India showed no awe or regard for imperialism's founders. This book provides a different account of the empire's greatness, the victories it provided to India, and the colonial past that differs from the history that many of us have studied. Tharoor presents a compelling argument for India and clarifies the exploitation committed by the British in India using facts and data. By dispelling the fallacy that India gained more from colonial authority than it lost, Tharoor exalts the history of the colonies.

Conclusion:

In "An Era of Darkness," Shashi Tharoor uncovers the injustices of British rule in India, depicting it as a dark period filled with suffering and poverty. Tharoor seeks acknowledgment and an apology for the enduring impact of British actions, emphasizing distress over reparations. A versatile figure in international service and politics, Tharoor explores post-colonial perspectives in works like "The Great Indian Novel" and "An Era of Darkness." He exposes British exploitation, discriminatory practices, and their impact on India's economy and education. Tharoor's narrative challenges traditional historical views, urging a nuanced understanding of India's colonial past. Through his post-colonial lens, the book contributes to reassessing history, dispelling myths, and fostering a more informed view of India's colonial legacy.

Works Cited

Durant, Will. The Case for India. Strand Book Stall, 2007

Ganie Tahi Mohd. "Review of An Era of Darkness." Aleph Book Company, 2018, pp. 1-7.

Justine, Sebin. "Shashi Tharoor's An Era of Darkness: The British Empire: Text and Context."International Journal of English Language, Literature in Humanities 7.4 (2019): 345-356.

Nimiwat, Dushyant. "Contemporary Critics and Critical Theories." Bareilly: Except Quotations from Elsewhere, 2017. Document.

Sharma, Saksham. "Book Review of the Era of Darkness" (DOC) Book Review of The Era of Darkness, Saksham Sharma -Academia.edu.

Tharoor, Shashi. An Era of Darkness. Rupa Publications India, 2016.

The Interconnectedness between the Individual Self and the Wider World: Arundhathi Subramaniam's *When God is a Traveller*

Ms. S. Sreepa

Assistant Professor, Department of English
VLB Janakiammal College of Arts and Science

The tranquil poetry and introspective themes in Arundhathi Subramaniam's *When God is a Traveller* take readers on a life-changing voyage of inquiry and self-discovery. Here's how this voyage is made easier by the collection:

The collection's poems explore spiritual issues, inviting readers to reflect on the purpose of life, the nature of existence, and one's relationship to the divine. Readers are invited to explore their own spiritual views and set off on a voyage of discovery by means of thoughtful writing and inquiry.

Throughout the collection, nature is a source of inspiration and introspection. Subramaniam creates an atmosphere of awe and admiration for the intricacy and beauty of the natural world by connecting readers with it through sensory descriptions and evocative imagery. Readers are inspired to consider their own relationship with nature and find comfort in its cycles and rhythms as a result of this connection with it.

The poems examine the nuances of romantic love, ties to one's family, and interactions with other people. Readers are invited to consider their own intimate, longing, and loving experiences via thoughtful poetry, which helps them gain a better knowledge of who they are and how they relate to other people.

As implied by the title, *When God is a Traveller* the main theme revolves around travel and discovery. Readers are guided on a voyage of self-discovery as they traverse the terrains of memory, time, and the inner self throughout the anthology. Readers examine their own identities, beliefs, and emotions through introspection and reflection, which promotes personal development and transformation.

Subramaniam offers comments on politics, inequality, and the human condition in his poetry, which also addresses more general society themes. Readers are invited to focus on their positions in society and how their behaviors and ideas relate to wider societal systems through astute observations and insightful analysis.

Subramaniam frequently explores the interconnection between the individual ego and the divine or cosmic forces in her poetry, delving into themes of spirituality and transcendence. She might consider how a person's spiritual experiences and beliefs affect how they view the world and their role in it.

The relationship between the unique self and larger cultural or historical backgrounds may also be explored in Subramaniam's poetry. She might examine how customs, cultural influences, and collective histories create individual identities, highlighting the relationship between individual experiences and broader societal narratives.

Subramaniam's poetry usually takes a global viewpoint, examining how humans are related to one another despite differences in geography and culture. In an increasingly interconnected society, she might investigate topics of globalization, migration, and interconnection.

The way that Arundhathi Subramaniam's *When God is a Traveller* affects a reader's emotions is highly individualized. Awe and wonder, introspection and self-reflection, empathy and compassion, transcendence and spiritual insight, sorrow and meditation, are, however, prevalent emotional themes. When reading Subramaniam's poetry, readers may feel a variety of feelings, from profound epiphanies and moments of inspiration to thoughtful reflection and emotional resonance with the poems' themes.

References:

https://books.google.co.in/books/about/When_God_Is_
    A_Traveller.html?id=L-
    XADwAAQBAJ&redir_esc=y

https://www.everand.com/book/445735726/When-God-
    Is-A-Traveller

https://www.kobo.com/in/en/ebook/when-god-is-a-
    traveller-1

Womanism Circumnavigating With Tradition and Modernity in *"Disorderly Women"* by Malathi Rao

Ms. Anjala Surya

Assistant Professor
Department of English
Sri Krishna Adithya College of Arts and Science, Coimbatore

Introduction

"Disorderly Women" by Malathi Rao stands as a profound exploration of the female experience in India, spanning generations and delving deep into the complexities of tradition, modernity, and the quest for self-determination. Through the lens of diverse characters, Rao crafts a narrative that not only depicts the struggles and triumphs of women but also interrogates the societal structures that shape and constrain their lives. This essay aims to unravel the workings of Rao's portrayal of tradition and modernity in "Disorderly Women," examining how these themes intersect with the characters' journeys towards autonomy and self-realization.

Tradition vs. Modernity: A Clash Explored

At the heart of "Disorderly Women" lies the tension between tradition and modernity, a dichotomy that permeates the lives of the novel's protagonists. Rao skillfully juxtaposes traditional values and customs with the forces of modernization, inviting readers to contemplate the ways in which these opposing forces shape the lives and choices of women in India.

The novel's opening introduces us to characters deeply rooted in tradition, such as the matriarchal figure who embodies the values of duty, sacrifice, and obedience to familial expectations. Through her experiences and interactions, Rao establishes the entrenched patriarchal norms that govern women's lives, dictating their roles within the family and society at large.

However, as the narrative unfolds, we witness the gradual encroachment of modernity into the characters' lives, challenging established norms and prompting questions about identity, agency, and self-expression. The younger generation, particularly the female protagonists, grapple with the tensions between tradition and modernity as they navigate their evolving roles in a rapidly changing world. Rao deftly portrays the conflicts that arise when traditional expectations clash with desires for autonomy and fulfillment, highlighting the complexities of negotiating identity within shifting cultural landscapes.

Marriage and Domesticity

One of the most prevalent themes in the novel is the pressure on women to conform to traditional gender roles, particularly in the context of marriage and domesticity. The older generation of women, influenced by traditional values, often view marriage as the ultimate goal for their daughters, emphasizing the importance of obedience and submission to their husbands. However, the younger generation challenges these expectations, seeking independence, education, and careers outside the home. For example, the character of Meera, a young woman determined to pursue her passion for literature despite her family's objections, symbolizes the clash between tradition and modernity in the realm of marriage and domesticity. *"She felt the weight of tradition pressing down on her, dictating every aspect of her life, from the clothes she wore to the dreams she dared to dream"* (Rao, p. 25).

Education and Empowerment

Another area where tradition and modernity intersect in the novel is in the characters' attitudes towards education and female empowerment. While traditional values prioritize domestic skills and obedience over formal education for women, modernity brings with it a growing awareness of the importance of education in empowering women to pursue their goals and aspirations. Characters like Maya, who defy societal expectations by pursuing higher education and professional careers, serve as catalysts for change, challenging the traditional notion that a woman's place is solely within the confines of the home.

Sexuality and Freedom

Rao also explores the theme of female sexuality and freedom in "Disorderly Women," shedding light on the ways in which tradition and modernity shape women's attitudes towards their bodies and desires. Traditional values often repress female sexuality, viewing it as something to be controlled and regulated within the confines of marriage. However, modernity challenges these restrictive norms, advocating for women's right to sexual autonomy and bodily integrity. Characters like Leela, who rebel against societal expectations by embracing their sexuality and asserting their right to pleasure, symbolize the struggle for freedom and selfexpression in a patriarchal society. *"She refused to be silenced, her voice ringing out against the injustices of a patriarchal society that sought to suppress her every word and deed"* (Rao, p.205).

The Quest for Female Self-Determination

Central to "Disorderly Women" is the protagonists' relentless pursuit of female self-determination, a journey fraught with obstacles yet imbued with resilience, courage, and resilience. Rao's characters defy societal expectations and carve out their own paths, challenging conventional notions of womanhood and asserting their right to autonomy.

Each character's journey towards self-determination is unique, shaped by personal experiences, societal pressures, and the interplay between tradition and modernity. Through their struggles and triumphs, Rao underscores the importance of agency and self-empowerment in the face of adversity, inspiring readers to contemplate the possibilities and limitations of female autonomy in patriarchal societies. *"They said a woman's place was in the home, but she knew her ambitions stretched far beyond the confines of domesticity"* (Rao, p. 112).

Intersectionality and Diversity

"Disorderly Women" also explores the intersectionality of identity and the diverse experiences of women within Indian society. The novel features characters from different backgrounds, castes, and socio-economic statuses, each navigating their own unique struggles and challenges. Through their stories, the author highlights the interconnectedness of gender, class, caste, and other social factors, illustrating how these intersecting identities shape women's lives in complex ways. By centering diverse voices and experiences, "Disorderly Women" offers a rich and nuanced portrayal of the multifaceted nature of female identity and agency in India.

The Legacy of Tradition and the Imperative of Change

At its core, "Disorderly Women" grapples with the legacy of tradition and the imperative of change in Indian society. The novel depicts the tension between the desire to uphold cultural heritage and the need to challenge oppressive norms and practices. While tradition provides a sense of stability and belonging for some characters, it also serves as a source of constraint and limitation, particularly for women seeking autonomy and self-expression. As the younger generation comes of age, they confront the contradictions and injustices inherent in traditional gender roles, inspiring them to question, resist, and ultimately reshape the norms that govern their lives. In doing so, they embody the spirit of progress and transformation, paving the way for a more inclusive and equitable society.

Celebrating the Complexity of Women's Lives

In "Disorderly Women," Malathi Rao offers a vivid and poignant portrayal of women's lives in India, celebrating their resilience, courage, and unwavering spirit in the face of adversity. Through richly drawn characters, nuanced storytelling, and thought-provoking themes, the novel invites readers to contemplate the complexities of female identity and agency within a patriarchal society. From the bonds of sisterhood to the challenges of tradition and modernity, "Disorderly Women" speaks to the universal struggles and triumphs of women everywhere, reminding us of the power of solidarity, resistance, and the relentless pursuit of self-determination. In celebrating the diversity and complexity of women's experiences, "Disorderly Women" reaffirms the importance of amplifying diverse voices and narratives in literature and beyond, inspiring us to envision a world where every woman can thrive and flourish on her own terms.

In "Disorderly Women" by Malathi Rao, the themes and narratives present resonate with aspects of womanism, a concept that emphasizes the intersectionality of race, class, and gender, particularly focusing on the experiences and struggles of Black women. While the novel may not explicitly engage with womanism as a theoretical framework, it does explore similar themes of female empowerment, solidarity, and resistance against oppressive systems.

Womanism acknowledges the multiple layers of identity that influence a woman's experience, including race, class, and gender. Similarly, "Disorderly Women" portrays a diverse range of female characters who navigate intersecting social and cultural factors that shape their lives. These characters come from various backgrounds and face different challenges based on factors such as caste, socio-economic status, and regional differences. Through their stories, the novel underscores the importance of recognizing and addressing the complexities of women's experiences within Indian society.

Female Solidarity and Empowerment

Womanism places a strong emphasis on female solidarity and empowerment, advocating for the collective upliftment of women. In "Disorderly Women," we see instances of women coming together to support and uplift each other in the face of adversity. Whether it's through friendships, familial bonds, or community networks, the female characters in the novel find strength and resilience in their connections with one another. They challenge patriarchal norms and resist oppression through acts of solidarity, highlighting the transformative power of women's collective action.

Womanism critiques patriarchal structures and oppressive systems that perpetuate inequality and injustice, particularly for women of colour. Similarly, "Disorderly Women" offers a critical examination of patriarchal norms and traditions within Indian society. The novel exposes the ways in which women are marginalized, silenced, and constrained by societal expectations and gender roles. Through the characters' experiences and struggles, the author highlights the urgent need to dismantle patriarchal systems and create spaces for women to assert their autonomy and agency.

Conclusion

In "Disorderly Women," Malathi Rao offers a poignant exploration of tradition, modernity, and the quest for female self-determination in India. Through richly drawn characters and a compelling narrative, Rao invites readers to contemplate the complexities of women's lives in a patriarchal society, while celebrating their resilience, courage, and unwavering pursuit of autonomy. As the characters navigate the tensions between tradition and modernity, they remind us of the enduring strength and resilience of women in the face of adversity, inspiring us to envision a world where every woman can realize her full potential.

Work Cited

Rao Malathi. *Disorderly Women.* Mumbai: Dronequill Publishers, 2005. Print

https://epublications.marquette.edu/cgi/viewcontent.cgi?article=1211&context=lnq

https://www.ncbi.nlm.nih.gov/pmc/articles/PMC4381312/

Comparing the Poem of Jeet Thayil's These Error Are Correct With John O Donohue's For Grief in the Aspect of Grief, Love and Loss

Ms. E. Arulmozhinayaki

Assistant Professor, Department of English,
VLB Janakiammal College of Arts and Science, Coimbatore.

Introduction:

An Indian poet Jeet Thayil, who raised in 1959. He is the creator of several collection of poetry including *These Errors Are Correct* which was published in 2008 and won the Sahitya Akademi Award. His vast contributions to Literature and Arts have given him honours. Thayil's collection of work demonstrates his various artistic interests, which include poetry, fiction and music. His works of art often show a unique blend of cultural influences that are a reflection of what he believes and experiences. He has written three volumes of poetry. He dedicated this poetry to his beloved wife who left him alone in this existing world. This poem shares the emotional experience of Jeet towards his wife.

John O Donohue was an Irish poet, author, catholic priest and a philosopher. He was a native Irish speaker. O Donohue became well-known for his intellectual and literary writings. Themes like spirituality, love, nature and the fusion of Celtic wisdom and modern philosophy are often explored in his works. One of his notable poem *For Grief* illustrates how a man missed his loved after their death and their absence made the man's life empty.

Nature of Grief:

The poems start with acknowledging the universal nature of grief. Both the poets state Grief is an unexpected emotion that every human will experience once in their life. They considered the Grief as permanent stranger who embrace them very closely because both the poets were in the state of losing their beloved. Worrying about someone who left us is normal but worrying about the one who spend their whole life for the happiness of their family is not that much easy. In O'Donohue's *For Grief,*

When you lose someone you love,

Your life becomes strange, (For Grief, line1-2)

Paradoxical Emotions:

The poem examines the contradictory aspects of grief where grief and pain coexist with the possibility of change and growth. According to O'Donohue, grieving can force people to face their innermost feelings and take stock of their life.

It becomes hard to trust yourself.

All you can depend on now is that

Sorrow will remain faithful to itself,

(For Grief, line23-25)

In both the poems, we could realize the feeling of sorrow and pain which was experienced by the poets but that pain will give a remainder for them that they should come out of that grief and they should live their present life with the wonderful memories of their beloved. That feeling of Grief i.e. thinking or living with the memories of their spouse, gives them a pure happy and that was the medicine for their pain. So in these poems of *For Grief* and *These Errors are Correct,* there will be the mixture of emotions such as sorrow and happiness which take place in it.

Transformation of Loss:

> *Gradually, you will learn acquaintance*
>
> *With the invisible form of your departed;*

(For Grief, line 31-32)

The poems highlight that grieving is a journey that can result in significant transformation rather than just a procedure of tolerating the misery. The poems make a claim that there is a chance for introspection and rebirth even in the darkest moments. This transformation taught them that they should be lead their life independently and they were still living with their loved one in their own world called "Love". It trained them how to stand single and face all the obstacles by themselves.

Eternal Connection:

These poems place a significant focus on the universal nature of grief, underscoring the importance of coming together as a community amidst sorrow. The poems propose that by recognizing and expressing our grief alongside others, we can discover comfort and strength through a shared comprehension of the experience of loss. This perspective highlights the value of solidarity and empathy in navigating the often overwhelming emotions tied to bereavement. Even though the poets and their loved ones were separated by the term called "Death", "Loss of Life", "Demise", "Passing Away", etc.. but they were eternally connected by the label named as "Love". Only their physical appearance or the physique may disappear from this world, their love and soul were live in this existing world.

Conclusion:

In Jeet Thayil's *These errors are Correct* and John O Donohue's *For Grief,* we could sense that how a man feels for his beloved after her death. There is a saying, "Men are strong in physically, mentally and psychologically than women." Through these poetic lines, Thayil and O'Donohue exhibit that they may be physically strong but psychologically they were completely not strong because of the absence of their loved one.

Reference:

https://en.wikipedia.org/wiki/Jeet_Thayil

https://en.wikipedia.org/wiki/John_O%27Donohue

https://wordsfortheyear.com/2019/01/15/for-grief-by-john-odonohue/

https://www.goodreads.com/quotes/7960340-all-you-can-depend-on-now-is-that-sorrow-will

https://www.researchgate.net/publication/361606940_Personal_Grief_in_Jeet_Thayil's_These_Errors_are_Correct

https://www.youtube.com/watch?v=BWjJv9ZZik

A Study of Radical Feminism in Rupa Bajwa's *The Sari Shop*

Mr. K. Lakshmanan

PhD Research Scholar (Part -Time), Govt. Arts College (A), Coimbatore.

Introduction

Rupa Bajwa's novel *The Sari Shop* explores the journey of women from different social levels. It also reflects their unique role in society. The female characters go through varied situations. Rina Kapoor is Ravinder Kapoor's daughter, a prominent businessman in Amritsar. She has a master's degree in English literature and is an aspiring writer. Bajwa portrays Rina Kapoor as a well-read, upper-class woman. She knows what she expects from her life and is courageous enough to voice her feelings: *"I like to read, I like to explore new things, I like to take every day of life as a new experience ... I think life is an adventure. And when you explore life, you also explore yourself"* (TSS 81). She is very passionate about her writing and her still taking the time out for writing amidst the arrangements of marriage is clearly shows that:

> *... yesterday I wrote another poem. One of the poems in which I find that I can express the true meaning of life. And do you know when I wrote it? While a man who brought over crystal bangles for me to see was waiting outside. I felt the urge and I knew that bangles could wait, but I needed to get the creative process going. (TSS 81)*

As a woman Rina Kapoor faces gender discrimination. She is expected to follow certain norms that any woman is obliged to. She is even required to carry out her gender-specific responsibilities. Her father and society expect her to marry a wealthy man because she is from the upper class.

> *Ravinder Kapoor ... told the Guptas that his own daughter, Rina, was getting married in three weeks' time. He wasn't very pleased about it, because it was a Love Marriage, and his daughter had chosen to marry a Captain in the Indian Army. Ravinder Kapoor still couldn't believe it, but he had not tried not to let his disappointment show. (TSS 163)*

The society she belonged to expected her to stay within the four walls after her marriage. Rina Kapoor is able to pursue her aspirations because of her excellent social standing. Sometimes it is vital to evaluate an individual's experiences, whether positive or negative. Rina, a high class product with access to education, has her own voice. Rina did not want to be held in the control of society. Just three days after her marriage she visits the sari shop to try to find some exploration for her novel and gets succeeded in publishing her novel. Due to her high standing in society, she is able to make her novel prominent and also succeeds in drawing the attention of the people towards her book. Rina's status according to her gender is that of an oppressed woman, but according to her class is an oppressor.

Another female character in the novel is Mrs. Sachdeva, Head of the Department of English at a neighboring college. *"Really, Rina, now these people have started to come to our home also. We are friends with the highest status families in Amritsar . . . And just because of you, we have these ordinary, professor-type, service class women coming here"* (TSS 91). Mrs. Sachdeva, a middle-class woman, is victimized when upper-class women such as Mrs. Gupta criticize about her. Nonetheless, she has various opportunities to improve her career, pursue her passions, and live a life entirely under her control. It is important to evaluate both oppressions and privileges in order to really comprehend someone.

Another character is Kamla. She is very poor working-class, uneducated woman. Her father works in a factory, while her mother is a maid. After her mother's death, she begins to work as a maid to support the family. When she turns sixteen, her father marries her off to Chander, a factory worker. Kamla was not asked about her choice because she belonged to a less privileged sector of society. Chander, her husband, eventually loses his job and begins to drink and attack her. She was not allowed to work since her spouse wanted her to have children as soon as possible. Eventually, she does get pregnant and she got some light of confidence enters her life. However, her miscarriage was caused by fate and a poor lifestyle. Her husband provided no assistance, and she was constantly blamed for everything that happened in their lives, including poverty and miscarriage. As a result, Kamla develops an alcohol addiction. She resorts to drinking and snapping at males in the neighbourhood. Obviously, the society accuses Kamla of everything. Even Chander's friend Gokul describes Kamla as *"not a good woman"* (TSS119).

However, Kamla quickly discovers that the real culprits in her life are Mr. Gupta and Mr. Kapoor. Chander was working in their factory, and when the factory was losing money, they simply stopped it without paying the workers' salaries for the previous three months. All of these contributed to Chander's household poverty and Kamla's miscarriage. Kamla, enraged and inebriated, throws stones at Mr. Gupta's house and screams insults, resulting in her detention. The police constables rape her inside the police station. She is reckless due to her circumstances.

Conclusion

All the female characters in the novel The Sari Shop face gender oppression, irrespective of their position, social class, and education. The study explores the female characters intersectional experiences, exploring how gender-based oppression connects with class, power, and societal standards. Through a radical feminist lens, the paper illuminates the complexities of patriarchy, women's agency, and the pursuit of liberation in the context of contemporary Indian society depicted in the novel. It covers the themes of patriarchy, gender oppression, and women's agency, offering a thorough analysis of the novel from a radical feminist perspective.

Works Cited:

Bajwa, Rupa. *The Sari Shop*. Penguin Books, 2004.

Cottais, Camille. Radical Feminism Written by Camille Cottais Translated by Caroline Feldner 1. Definition Context of Emergence. 2021. https://igg-geo.org/wp-content/uploads/2021/04/Technical-Sheet-Radical-feminism.pdf

Magotra, Dr Sheweta. Women and Class Struggle: A Marxist Feminist Perspective in the Sari Shop by Rupa Bajwa. Elementary Education Online, vol. 20, no. 2, 23 June 2022, pp. 2169.

Confronting Childhood Trauma: A Study of Maternal Abandonment in Anuradha Roy's *All the Lives We Never Lived*

Ms. Nishanthine V

Ph.D. Scholar (Part Time), Department of English, Government Arts College, Coimbatore.

Throughout history, humanity has been embroiled in various wars, highlighting the stark realities of warfare. Initially, warfare served as a catalyst for traumatic events and was considered an integral aspect of civilization, as human survival often seemed contingent upon it. This notion was subsequently elaborated upon by numerous theorists. For instance, Thomas Hobbes, in Leviathan, articulates, *"I posit a universal inclination among all people toward an incessant and restless pursuit of power, a pursuit that ceases only upon death."* Additionally, he contends that *"those who possess the greatest power, namely kings, direct their efforts towards securing it domestically through legislation or internationally through warfare. Once achieved, a new desire emerges: for some, it is the pursuit of fame through further conquests; for others, it is the pursuit of comfort and hedonistic pleasures; and for yet others, it is the desire for recognition or praise for excellence in various arts or intellectual abilities."*

The evolution of warfare throughout history has been intertwined with the progression of civilization, giving rise to phenomena such as imperialism, colonialism, and the dominance of certain cultural norms. However, along with these developments came the legacy of colonial trauma, epitomized by instances like the Holocaust, and the enduring effects of survival trauma. As societies advanced into the era of modernity, marked by scientific breakthroughs and infrastructural advancements, new discoveries reshaped the human experience. Industrialization and the expansion of railway networks brought about both advantages and drawbacks. While these advancements facilitated progress and economic growth, they also ushered in a new era of risks, including an increase in industrial accidents resulting in untimely deaths and widespread trauma. The advent of modern technology further accentuated this duality, offering both positive advancements and negative consequences. While modernity brought about improvements in various aspects of human life, it also introduced anthropogenic activities that disrupted ecosystems, accelerated industrialization, and contributed to environmental degradation. Consequently, this complex interplay between progress and its repercussions has given rise to instances of human suffering and traumatic events, reflecting the multifaceted nature of societal evolution.

The term 'trauma' originates from the Greek word meaning 'wound.' Initially, it referred solely to physical injuries, but over time, its definition expanded to encompass psychological wounds as well. Trauma is a complex phenomenon that encompasses various dimensions, including historical, sociological, and cultural aspects. While the Greeks primarily associated trauma with bodily harm, contemporary understanding acknowledges its profound impact on mental health. We now recognize that the effects of psychological trauma can persist long after physical wounds have healed. Post-traumatic stress disorder (PTSD) is a well-established psychological response to traumatic experiences, characterized by symptoms such as depression, anxiety, flashbacks, and recurrent nightmares. These symptoms often arise following intensely stressful events like warfare, natural disasters, or instances of sexual or physical abuse. Understanding the psychological ramifications of trauma is crucial for providing effective support and intervention for those affected by such experiences.

The exploration of trauma as a concept began in the 17th century, primarily focusing on its physical manifestations. However, as psychology and psychoanalysis evolved over time, trauma acquired deeper dimensions and complexities. It came to be understood not only as a physical reality but also as an event that induces distress, disharmony, shock, suffering, and pain. Additionally, trauma can lead to disassociation and fragmentation of one's sense of self. Individuals in a state of trauma may experience various symptoms such as hallucinations, flashbacks, nightmares, and overwhelming feelings of repression and distress.

Moreover, the experience of trauma blurs the traditional boundaries between various dichotomies, such as mind and body, memory and forgetting, speech and silence, inward and outward expressions, private and public spheres, and individual and collective experiences. Judith Herman, a renowned neurologist, elaborates on this complexity in her book "Trauma and Recovery." Through her work, she emphasizes how trauma transcends mere physical injury, affecting every aspect of an individual's existence and challenging conventional understandings of human psychology and societal norms.

The study of psychological trauma has a curious history—one of episodic amnesia. Periods of active investigation have alternated with periods of oblivion. Repeatedly in the past century, similar lines of inquiry have been taken up and abruptly abandoned, only to be rediscovered much later. Classic documents of fifty or one hundred years ago often read like contemporary works. Though the field has in fact an abundant and rich tradition, it has been periodically forgotten and must be periodically reclaimed.

Psychiatry is a specialized medical field dedicated to diagnosing and treating mental illnesses, recognizing their pathological nature. Conversely, psychoanalysis delves into the intricate workings of the human psyche, exploring aspects such as cognition, consciousness, perception, knowledge, desires, instincts, emotions, and the subconscious.

The advent of psychology as a formal discipline in the 19th century marked a significant shift in medical science's approach to understanding the human mind. Prior to this, the focus had primarily been on physical ailments. However, with the emergence of psychology, medical professionals began to delve into the complexities of mental health.

Jean-Martin Charcot, a prominent French neurologist, played a pivotal role in bridging the gap between physical injuries and psychological disorders. Through his research, he observed the manifestation of psychological disturbances, such as aphasia and amnesia, resulting from physical trauma. This exploration eventually led to the recognition of conditions like hysteria, particularly prevalent among individuals experiencing shell shock during wartime.

Hysteria, characterized by various physical and emotional symptoms, provided a window into the unconscious mind. Neurologists discovered that traumatic experiences often lay buried within the depths of the subconscious, prompting further exploration into the connections between these experiences and pathological behaviors. This exploration laid the groundwork for the development of psychoanalytic techniques aimed at unraveling the complexities of the human psyche and addressing underlying trauma.

Trauma studies began to gain traction in the 1990s, initially rooted in Freudian theory. Drawing on Freud's insights, scholars explored trauma as a field of study that provided a framework for understanding the expression of the unconscious mind. Through systematic inquiry, researchers sought to comprehend the intricate dynamics of traumatic experiences and their impact on memory.

Freud's collaboration with Josef Breuer resulted in the seminal work "Studies on Hysteria," which laid the foundation for the study of trauma. In this influential text, they assert that while the actual encounter with a traumatic event may not be inherently traumatizing, its subsequent recollection can elicit profound distress. This insight paved the way for further exploration into the mechanisms underlying traumatic memory.

Expanding on his earlier work, Freud delved deeper into the concept of trauma in his essay "Beyond the Pleasure Principle." Here, he conceptualizes trauma as a defense mechanism of the ego, elucidating its role in shaping the psyche. Freud's exploration of trauma highlights its dual nature as both the origin and consequence of psychological distress, shedding light on the intricate interplay between traumatic experiences and the human psyche.

The emergence of trauma theory within literary criticism gained significant traction in 1996 with the publication of Cathy Caruth's seminal work, "Unclaimed Experiences: Trauma, Narrative, and History." Caruth's contributions to trauma studies have been profoundly influential, laying the groundwork for the widespread recognition and exploration of trauma within academic discourse. "Unclaimed Experiences" is widely regarded as a foundational text that propelled the field of trauma studies into the forefront of contemporary theoretical discourse.

In her book's introduction, Caruth elucidates the complex nature of trauma, asserting that it cannot be simply located within the initial violent or traumatic event experienced by an individual. Instead, she posits that trauma resides in the unassimilated aspects of the experience, those elements that were not fully comprehended or processed at the time of occurrence. These unresolved aspects of trauma often resurface later in the survivor's life, haunting them in unforeseen ways.

Today, trauma studies encompass a diverse and expansive discipline that engages scholars from various fields, including literature, psychology, philosophy, and history. The field continues to evolve, attracting attention from theorists, researchers, and historians who grapple with the complexities of trauma and its enduring impact on individuals and societies. Caruth's insights have served as a catalyst for ongoing exploration and analysis within this dynamic and multifaceted field of study.

Amidst a world grappling with an array of humanitarian, political, and ecological crises, the prevalence of both physical and psychological trauma has become all too common. These crises often spiral into prolonged and multifaceted experiences of suffering, disproportionately affecting certain environments and populations worldwide. Particularly in the global South, where a significant portion of the world's population resides, factors such as conflict, poverty, displacement, and disenfranchisement significantly increase the likelihood of experiencing trauma.

Despite the widespread prevalence of trauma in these regions, the majority of research and scholarly discourse on the topic originates from the global North. This imbalance in representation raises concerns about the extent to which the realities, contexts, and needs of trauma survivors in the global South are accurately understood and adequately addressed. Furthermore, existing literature often fails to capture the nuanced layers of disempowerment experienced by marginalized communities, particularly women of color, who are disproportionately subjected to various forms of sustained and systemic violence.

As a result, the voices of these marginalized groups are often muted in discussions surrounding trauma documentation and intervention, undermining the agency of survivors. The failure to fully recognize and amplify the experiences of those most affected by trauma hampers efforts to develop inclusive and effective approaches to trauma management and recovery on a global scale.

Anuradha Roy, a versatile author known for her proficiency across various literary genres, including novels, journalism, and editing, recently received the prestigious Sahitya Akademi Award in 2022 for her remarkable work "All the Lives We Never Lived." Unlike some of her previous works that depict external violence, death, and societal estrangement as catalysts for familial disintegration, this particular novel takes a different approach.

In "All the Lives We Never Lived" (2018), Roy portrays the trauma of familial dissolution through the lens of the protagonist's loss of his mother, Gayatri, who chooses to flee from their home environment, marked by oppressive patriarchal dominance. Rather than external factors directly causing the family's fracture, it is Gayatri's deliberate departure that serves as the intricate catalyst for their painful separation.

Gayatri's purposeful absence from the family unit is portrayed as a complex trigger, stemming from her desire to escape the confines of patriarchal oppression. However, this intentional separation initiates a profound emotional and psychological upheaval within the protagonist and the family dynamic as a whole. The protagonist's sense of identity and belonging are abruptly disrupted, leading to a series of disintegrative events that unravel the fabric of their existence.

Through her nuanced portrayal of familial rupture, Roy explores the complexities of human relationships and the repercussions of societal constraints on individual agency. The novel delves into the profound impact of personal choices on familial bonds, highlighting the intricate interplay between autonomy, survival, and emotional well-being in the face of adversity.

In their article titled "Quest for self in the novel 'All the Lives We Never Lived' by Anuradha Roy," K. Suganya and A. Selvaraj discuss the evolving roles of women in society. Drawing on Betty Friedan's seminal work, "The Feminine Mystique," they highlight the importance of women discovering their passions as a means to assert their own identities. According to Suganya and Selvaraj, Anuradha Roy's novel "All the Lives We Never Lived" encapsulates this notion of women's pursuit of self-identity.

The authors analyze Roy's text through the lens of women's autonomy and the imperative for women to prioritize their own needs and desires. They argue that the novel serves as a powerful exploration of the complexities surrounding women's identities and the challenges they face in asserting their agency within patriarchal structures.

By emphasizing the theme of self-discovery and empowerment, Suganya and Selvaraj underscore the significance of women's autonomy in shaping their own destinies. Through their analysis, they shed light on the broader societal implications of women's struggles for self-fulfillment and the ongoing quest for gender equality.

In his article "Memory and Loss in Anuradha Roy's 'All the Lives We Never Lived,'" Shailendra P. Singh delves into the narrative structure of the novel, highlighting how Anuradha Roy skillfully infuses the anxieties of the protagonist, Myshkin, and his mother, Gayatri, throughout the story. Singh draws attention to the thematic resonance of memory and loss within the narrative, drawing parallels to the works of acclaimed authors such as Salman Rushdie and Gabriel Garcia Marquez.

Singh underscores the significance of memory as a potent tool for constructing knowledge and understanding history, contrasting it with the Western emphasis on empirical evidence and rationality. He argues that while Western scientific traditions often downplay the value of memory in reconstructing historical events, non-Western narratives assert the validity of memory as an epistemological tool in its own right.

Through his analysis, Singh situates Anuradha Roy's novel within the broader context of literary works that explore the intersection of memory, history, and personal narrative. By foregrounding the characters' anxieties and the role of memory in shaping their experiences, Roy invites readers to contemplate the subjective nature of truth and the ways in which memory can illuminate hidden dimensions of the past.

In his research paper titled "Rejecting 'the Feminine Mystique' in Quest for Self-fulfillment: A Study of Meena Kandasamy's 'When I Hit you: Or, A Portrait of the Writer as a Young Wife' and Anuradha Roy's 'All the Lives We Never Lived,'" Tuhin Shuvra Sen explores how Anuradha Roy tackles pressing issues related to outdated notions of femininity and entrenched cultural norms that perpetuate male dominance in Indian society. Sen argues that Roy's work sheds light on the challenges faced by women as they navigate between societal expectations of subordination to men and their own aspirations for self-assertion and empowerment.

Sen emphasizes the dichotomous nature of a woman's existence, caught between the societal pressure to conform to masculine ideals and her desire to assert her own identity. Specifically focusing on the character of Gayatri as a married woman, Sen highlights the inherent struggle of being confined to roles as a wife and mother without opportunities to establish individual autonomy.

Through Sen's analysis, Roy's portrayal of female characters in "All the Lives We Never Lived" serves as a poignant commentary on the complexities of womanhood within the patriarchal framework of Indian society. Sen's exploration underscores the importance of challenging traditional gender norms and advocating for women's agency and self-fulfillment in the face of societal constraints.

In the opening of the novel "All the Lives We Never Lived," the protagonist, a young boy, introduces himself as "the boy whose mother had run off with an Englishman." This statement sets the tone for the narrative, highlighting the central theme of maternal abandonment and its profound impact on the protagonist's life. Gayatri, the boy's mother, inadvertently leaves him behind due to the oppressive influence of patriarchal domination within their society.

The sudden departure of his mother leaves a deep emotional scar on the young protagonist, Myshkin, resulting in a traumatic experience that shapes his childhood and beyond. The stigma and shame associated with his mother's actions further exacerbate Myshkin's sense of loss, as societal judgment becomes intertwined with his personal grief. This abandonment becomes a defining aspect of Myshkin's identity, overshadowing other aspects of his life. The social stigma surrounding his mother's departure permeates every aspect of Myshkin's existence, leaving him with a profound sense of isolation and division.

The permanence of this separation becomes evident in Myshkin's fragmented perspective of his life, where events are categorized based on their relation to his mother's departure. This constant reminder of the absence of his mother underscores the irrevocable nature of the loss and its enduring impact on Myshkin's psyche.

Even his interactions with his grandfather are colored by this separation, as questions about the timing of events serve as painful reminders of the before and after of his mother's departure. This poignant detail illustrates the profound and lasting effects of maternal abandonment on Myshkin's life, highlighting the complexities of navigating familial relationships amidst societal expectations and personal trauma.

The early loss of his mother had a profound and lasting impact on Myshkin. Growing up, he became increasingly introverted, longing for his mother's return while grappling with the unanswered questions surrounding her abandonment. It wasn't until he received a package of letters from his grandmother, detailing Gayatri's motivations for leaving, that he gained insight into her actions. Despite the prevailing assumption that Gayatri had abandoned her family for love, the letters revealed a different truth.

According to Gayatri's correspondence, her departure was not driven by romantic entanglement but rather by a desire to pursue her artistic passions and reclaim a sense of agency in her life. However, in order to embark on this journey of self-discovery, she felt compelled to leave behind her nine-year-old son, Myshkin, a decision that would haunt him for years to come. Myshkin struggled to come to terms with his mother's abandonment, burying his pain and memories of the scandalous episode deep within himself.

It wasn't until he stumbled upon his mother's letters that Myshkin realized the importance of confronting his past in order to find closure and peace. Through these revelations, he began to unravel the complexities of his mother's life and the societal pressures that shaped her decisions. Myshkin's journey of self-discovery also shed light on the systemic injustices faced by women in Indian society, leading him to reevaluate his understanding of his mother's actions and the broader cultural context in which they occurred.

The abrupt departure of his mother left Myshkin deeply traumatized, prompting existential questions to surface within him. In the wake of this profound loss, he found himself grappling with a sense of profound emptiness and a nagging uncertainty about his own existence. Myshkin's anguish was compounded by the realization that certain aspects of his life were irrevocably altered by his mother's departure, leaving indelible marks upon his psyche.

In his narration, Myshkin reflects on the enduring impact of his mother's absence, acknowledging the presence of lingering scars that refuse to fade with time. These emotional wounds serve as constant reminders of the pain and upheaval caused by his mother's sudden departure. Despite his efforts to move forward, Myshkin finds himself tethered to the past by these unshakeable memories and feelings of abandonment. As Myshkin navigates the complexities of grief and loss, he confronts the harsh reality that some experiences are so deeply ingrained within him that they become inseparable from his sense of self. Through his introspection, Myshkin grapples with the profound implications of his mother's absence, seeking solace amidst the turmoil of his fractured existence.

As a child, I would place my back against one of our trees and feel its reassuring solidity, its immobility. It was not going to move, it would never go anywhere, it was rooted to its spot. For as long as they are alive, trees remain where they are. This is one of life's few certainties. The roots of trees go deep and take many directions, we cannot foresee their subterranean spread any more than we can predict how a child will grow. Beneath the earth, trees live their secret lives, at times going deeper into the ground than up into the sky, entwined below with other trees which appear in no way connected above the ground (82).

Not only was Myshkin abandoned by his mother, Gayatri, but his father, Nek Chand, also left home to immerse himself in the freedom movement. Both parents, driven by their respective quests for freedom – one personal, the other national – left behind their nine-year-old son. Myshkin, grappling with the profound sense of loss and betrayal resulting from his parents' actions, likened people to trees, observing that while people possess the ability to uproot and depart, trees remain steadfast and enduring.

The trauma of abandonment profoundly influenced Myshkin's outlook on life, shaping his decisions and relationships in significant ways. The pain of being deserted by those closest to him instilled in him a deep-seated reluctance to form attachments or commitments that could potentially lead to further heartache. As a result, Myshkin chose to forgo marriage and instead devoted himself entirely to his passion for nature.

Finding solace in the permanence and tranquility of the natural world, Myshkin embarked on a career as a horticulturist, cultivating a deep connection with the land and its inhabitants. Through his work, he sought to create a sense of stability and continuity, counteracting the tumultuousness of his own upbringing. Myshkin's devotion to nature served as both a refuge from his past traumas and a means of finding purpose and fulfillment in a world marked by impermanence and upheaval.

The narrative of "All the Lives We Never Lived" revolves primarily around the intertwined lives of Gayatri and Myshkin. Gayatri emerges as a bold and determined woman who refuses to be confined by societal expectations, instead aspiring to carve out her own identity and pursue her passions. In contrast, Myshkin is depicted as a sensitive and introverted child who grapples with the profound loss of his mother at a tender age, leaving him feeling helpless and adrift.

Gayatri's character is defined by her relentless pursuit of personal freedom and self-expression. She defies traditional gender roles and societal norms, opting to abandon her familial responsibilities in favor of pursuing her own desires and ambitions. Her decision to prioritize her own autonomy and aspirations, even at the expense of her maternal duties, underscores her courage and determination to live life on her own terms.

However, while Gayatri's actions may be viewed as bold and empowering, they also have profound implications for Myshkin, whose childhood trauma reverberates throughout his life. The novel poignantly explores the lasting impact of maternal abandonment on Myshkin's emotional well-being and psychological development, illustrating how early experiences of loss can shape an individual's future trajectory.

Indeed, the novel delves into the universal phenomenon of cause and effect, highlighting how trauma can manifest unexpectedly in the lives of individuals, regardless of age or circumstance. Myshkin's traumatic experiences serve as a sobering reminder of the fragility of human existence and the enduring legacy of past wounds. Through the lens of Gayatri and Myshkin's intertwined narratives, the novel offers a poignant exploration of the complexities of freedom, identity, and the profound human capacity for resilience in the face of adversity.

Works cited

Abrahams, Hilary. *Supporting Women after Domestic Violence : Loss, Trauma and Recovery*. Philadelphia, Jessica Kingsley Publishers, 2007.

Breuer, Josef, et al. *Studies on Hysteria*. New York, Basic Books, 2000.

Caruth, Cathy. *Trauma: Explorations in Memory*. Baltimore, Johns Hopkins University Press, 1995.

Caruth, Cathy. *Unclaimed Experience : Trauma, Narrative, and History*. Baltimore, Johns Hopkins University Press, 1996.

Casper, Monica J, and Eric Wertheimer. *Critical Trauma Studies Understanding Violence, Conflict and Memory in Everyday Life*. New York; London New York University Press, 2016.

Fletcher, John. *Freud and the Scene of Trauma*. Fordham Univ Press, 2 Dec. 2013.

Roy, Anuradha. *All the Lives We Never Lived*. London Maclehose Press / Quercus, 2019.

Diasporic Feminism within the Postcolonial Gamut: A Study of Rebellious Return in the Story of Sunetra Gupta's *Memories of Rain*

Mr. Dhandapani A.
Ph.D. Research Scholar, Department of English (Aided),
Kongunadu Arts and Science College (Autonomous), Coimbatore

Dr. R. Sumathi
Assistant Professor, Department of English (Aided),
Kongunadu Arts and Science College (Autonomous), Coimbatore

Dr. P. Sujatha
Assistant Professor, Department of English (Aided),
Kongunadu Arts and Science College (Autonomous), Coimbatore

A considerable time has passed since the colonizers started to dominate and got a backlash rejection from the colonized and eventually led to the latter's independence. However, the interdependence continues even today as it is a globalized world now. The works of fiction, kind of, take this interdependence to the level of accusations upon the colonizers in order to define the colonized. And thus, the postcolonial theoretical perspectives spring up validating the colonized community's response and the identity formed out of it. In a way, the postcolonial attitude supports adopting the colonizers' culture and language in order to decentralise them. The diasporic migration from one's homeland to distant places of the colonized can even be viewed under this lens. The experience is to have a nostalgia about one's place of origin, when the roots have been left where they were.

Yet what drives the migration is interesting. The fascination towards something different and superiorly assertive has always been the root of all the intercultural contacts. The West, not just wanted to have a dominion in the East, but it is also drawn towards its fascinating, mystic, exotic and appealing ways of life and valuable virtues. Naturally man has always thought of making something beautiful to be solely entrapped in his possession. The fascination can be said mutual, that is, the East also has seen the West with wonder.

In the context of actual people involved, the binaries like the West and East not only took the roles of colonizer and colonized but also, in a gendered version, Man and Woman respectively. While the metaphors, man and woman apply to the West and East, the gender difference seems to play a great role even in local communities. The discourses about patriarchal dominance have been seriously contested and debated ones every day. But in a scenario when a man from the West courts a woman from the East, things flare up not only in the narrow contexts of gender but in broad contexts like intercultural turmoil, marital inconsistencies, feminism, identity crisis, postcolonialism, the need for diaspora, or even questioning the need for a diasporic experience.

The discussion of Sunetra Gupta's novel, *Memories of rain* will give way to a thought so as to question the need for a diasporic experience. It is not about the distrust but rather the meditation over the idea – what lacks in the homeland that makes a person migrate in search of hope and later feel sorry and extremely nostalgic. The female protagonist, Moni breaks the diasporic experience and sees her homeland, not only in her memories, but in person, in a new light of hope. The idea of return will make more sense after the analysis of certain key notions, events and actions in the story.

Moni's love life is the vortex of the entire novel's discursive promises. She is a passionate and a metaphorized symbolic package of the enticing and virtuous East in the eyes of her British husband, Anthony. Anthony sets foot in India as a student to learn not about just India, but to possess it in some form and that happens to be Moni. Moni has a defined sense of femininity that is marked by sensual and sexual satisfaction. She disregards her aunt, who gets divorced, and her teacher, who is single, for their wasteful lives not made moist by the touch of a man. However, she is passionate about a life of lovemaking and wishes to escape her homeland, Calcutta.

In her initial vision, Calcutta is marked by patriarchal dominance and the drudges of a middle-class marital life devoid of meaning. The very title has the element of rain, which she despises. The rain floods the streets and fills up the city's sewers and the damp climate of Calcutta often gives disgusting nausea to Moni. She longs to escape from its clutches and she sees Anthony as her rescuer. Anthony does not like Moni for who she is but for what she represents, the sensual exotic fantasy of the East. Like his ancestral colonizers he subtly wishes to devour the beauty of Calcutta through Moni. There are many images where India is equated with Moni, thus giving a scope for eco-feministic exploration in the novel.

But after she leaves Calcutta for the promising diasporic space of London, she is not welcomed the way she desired. It is hard for her to establish her feminine diasporic identity, since she is unable to reclaim her past. The past, in the form of Calcutta, is a hell she wants to escape and the only satisfaction she had is Tagore's poetry. This reminiscence makes it impossible for her neither to accept Calcutta nor to embrace the loveless and adulterous London manifested in the form of her husband, Anthony as he has an affair with Anna, a white woman. He brings Anna in a very close contact with Moni that she is mute and could not possibly express her concern over the adulterous relationship.

The memories of the disgusting and wreak havocking rain slowly reminds her of a long-lost lover in the form of Calcutta. In the narrative of the novel, Gupta talks about the weeping puddles when Moni left for London. Yet the gender of Calcutta is still feminine, which subverts the heteronormative dichotomy. At this juncture in the novel the colonialist dichotomy between Anthony and Moni is also visibly delineated. The author also talks about yet another childhood companion of Moni, that is, the element of darkness personified. The darkness even follows Moni to London where she commits an adulterous relationship with it, the fact of which is held in stark contrast with the affair her husband has. The theme of rebellion subtly starts to surface in the memories of Moni.

Eventually it is this darkness that saves Moni and makes her realise what she needs. Her identity, as she once thinks, is no longer defined by the experience of her body, but in a way beyond that – what fulfils her soul on the longer run. The diasporic space fails to comfort her female experience, nor does the former homeland space of Calcutta before she left. Now it is time for Moni to create a third space to nurture her fractured female identity. This is only possible when she makes Calcutta less despising and more nostalgic in her reminiscing process. By facilitating a return to the likable Calcutta negating its ugliness and finding comforts in its very culture that has given birth to her hero-poet, Tagore, Moni makes the diasporic migration circular.

The theme of rebellious return to the new space that appears promising, the Calcutta that Moni longs for in the present, is the only feministic view that might help women like Moni struggling in the diasporic space. It also happens to subvert the idea of interdependence that the colonized had with the colonizer, which in this case, Moni is no longer interdependent on Anthony or London.

Moni enters the phase where she realises that her feminine sensibility grows beyond her bodily aspirations and more towards the social domain. Just like her teacher who leaves her marital interests for her academic pursuits, Moni leaves the clutches of a tumultuous marital frame for a career as a charity worker. When she decides such things, she projects her identity into the realm of martyrdom. Not only she is a victim of a colonial marriage, but a survivor and a role model to subvert power clashes existing in binary relationships.

Despite developing affiliations with a western Whitewoman, Anthony, the Englishman does not wish to leave his colony, India seen represented through the image of Moni. Though he wants to have both of them, the lenses with which he sees them are completely different. With Moni and her India, it has always been a colonizer's gaze to conquer and possess or that of a white tourist's awe to fancy the exotic east and bring home an eastern souvenir, which is Moni by the way. This objectification of Moni's femininity is detrimental to her, making it difficult for her to have a unique identity of her own. So, she decides to foster the identity in a more conducive environment. Though the idea that Calcutta is not so promising, as seen from her earlier memories, she makes it promising only through a diasporic escape and initiating the thought of return.

In many diasporic experiences, the possibility of return is hardly a thing. But it can be said that the question of the need for a diasporic experience is to make the homeland more palatable and escaping its antisocial structures at the crucial moment. In Moni's story, if she had stayed in Calcutta, she would have been caught in the drudgery of marriage where she would have worked as a teacher in the local school dusting the brassware on a gloomy afternoon in tears when her husband drags her drunk brother out of the house. But now the diasporic experience has provided a temporary relief from the setup of marriage and to revision her future life with a remarkable identity of her own.

As the novel ends with Moni's return, she nostalgically contemplates about the sky while riding in a taxi. She also could hear the tune of her Tagore's song in a child's voice which appears to be promising. The wheels of the taxi crush a crow's carcass more onto the tar road, symbolising the postcolonial overthrow of the colonial oppression. She witnesses the burst of a water main, symbolising a rejuvenating experience – washing away her diaspora and bringing a sunshine into her feminine sensibility.

Works Cited:

Banerjee, Bidisha. "Revisions, Reroutings and Return: Reversing theTeleology of Diaspora in Sunetra Gupta's *Memories of Rain." Postcolonial Text*, vol. 5, no.2, 2009.

Gupta, Sunetra.*Memories of Rain*. Weidenfeld, 1992.

Jain, Neelu, and Rani Rathore. "Re-locating 'Home' Through Memories in Sunetra Gupta's *So Good in Black."Literary Endeavour*, vol. 9, no. 4, Oct, 2018, pp. 106-110.

Manjula, T. "Home Thoughts from Abroad: A study of SunetraGupta's *Memories of Rain* and A Sin of Colour." Journal of Emerging Technologies and

Innovative Research, vol. 5, no. 11, Nov, 2018, pp. 541-544.

Sharma, Priya. "Burdensome Borders: A Diasporic Study of The Novel *Memories of Rain* by Sunetra Gupta." International Journal for Multidisciplinary Research, vol. 5, no. 5, 2023, pp. 1-6.

Sindhu, C, and N. S. Vishnu Priya. "Emancipation Of a Woman in Sunetra Gupta's *Memories of Rain.*" *Journal of Critical Reviews*, vol. 7, no. 14, 2020, pp. 147-149.

Thomas, Mercy. "Unveiling the Traumas of Intercultural Marriage in Sunetra Gupta's

Memories of Rain."International Journal of Creative Research Thoughts, vol. 6, no. 2, 2018, pp. 368-376.

Wankhade, D. B. "Alienation Approach in *Memories of Rain* of Sunetra Gupta." *LangLit*, Apr 2022, pp. 269-272.

Realising the Posthuman Subjectivity in Amit Chaudhuri's "Going for a Drive" – A Critical Analysis

Dr N. C. Vethambal

Associate Professor (Rtd.)

Government Arts College (Autonomous), Coimbatore

Amit Chaudhuri is a contemporary poet known for his evocative explorations of memory and materiality in his poems. He captures the intricate interplay between human beings, machines, and the environment in his poem "Going For A Drive." The poem examines themes of nostalgia, interconnectedness, and the passage of time, situating the human experience within a broader, non-human context. With its rich sensory imagery and reflective tone, the work invites readers to question traditional notions of subjectivity and agency. By applying Rosi Braidotti's posthuman subjectivity theory, this article aims to reveal the poem's layered narrative and its meditation on the human-machine-environment relationship.

Rosi Braidotti's theory of posthuman subjectivity offers a compelling framework through which to analyze the poem "Going for a Drive." In her seminal work The Posthuman (2013), Braidotti presents the notion of a decentered human subjectivity, emphasizing the interconnectedness of humans, technology, and the environment. "Digital 'second life', genetically modified food, advanced prosthetics, robotics and reproductive technologies are familiar facets of our globally linked and technologically mediated societies. This has blurred the traditional distinction between the human and its others, exposing the non-naturalistic structure of the human" (Braidotti*Posthuman* 45).This relational ontology challenges anthropocentric hierarchies, proposing instead a view of humans as entangled with non-human entities, such as machines and the material world.

Braidotti's concept of relational ontology highlights the interconnectedness of humans and the material world, positing that subjectivity arises through relationships rather than existing as an isolated entity (Toffoletti 211). In "Going for a Drive," the car and its components are not mere objects but active participants in the speaker's experience, shaping their memories and emotions. For instance, the poem describes the car's internal mechanisms with visceral imagery: *"Young, I loved / that smell / of fuel washing the car-intestine, its suddenness, / its spontaneous personality"* (lines 14-17). Here, the metaphor of the "car-intestine" likens the vehicle to a living organism, establishing a profound connection between the human and machine. This relational perspective aligns with Braidotti's idea that humans and non-humans co-construct each other's existence.

The speaker's affection for the car's "spontaneous personality" further illustrates the car's agency in this relationship. It is not a static object but a dynamic entity that elicits emotional responses. The "bitter exactness" of petrol (line 19) and the "suddenness" of the car's mechanisms evoke sensory experiences that contribute to the speaker's sense of self. This interaction underscores Braidotti's argument that subjectivity emerges from relational entanglements with the non-human, challenging the notion of human autonomy.

Braidotti's emphasis on vital materiality posits that matter possesses a form of agency, challenging the traditional dichotomy between subject and object (Haynes 19). The poem reflects this perspective through its depiction of fuel and machinery as vibrant, almost sentient forces. The "sharp, bitter aura of petrol" (line 8) is described as "spontaneous" and imbued with personality, suggesting that the fuel's materiality shapes the speaker's experience as much as their own emotions do.

This agency is further emphasized in the depiction of *"every derelict / service station, or among ruined despondent engines, / or bleary pools in dumps / with rainbows / in their eyes"* (lines 20-24). The "rainbows in their eyes" evoke the iridescence of oil spills, transforming an industrial byproduct into something aesthetically evocative and alive. The imagery elevates these non-human elements to participants in the speaker's journey, resonating with Braidotti's notion that matter itself is vibrant and dynamic.

The speaker's nostalgia further reflects this entanglement with vital materiality. The poem's sensory descriptions of fuel, engines, and "bleary pools" suggest that the speaker's memories and emotional states are intimately tied to their interactions with the material world. This connection challenges anthropocentric notions of memory and emotion as exclusively human phenomena. Instead, the poem suggests that non-human matter plays a crucial role in shaping the speaker's subjectivity, aligning with Braidotti's assertion that the human self is co-constituted by its relationships with the material and technological worlds.

A key aspect of Braidotti'sposthuman subjectivity is the dissolution of boundaries between human and machine (Braidotti, "Affirmative" 179). In "Going for a Drive," this boundary blurring is evident in the speaker's intimate connection with the car. The description of "the dark cogs and the pistons" as "haunting" (line 26) imbues the machine with an almost ghostly presence, suggesting that the car is not merely a tool but an integral part of the speaker's identity. The car's "dark" interior and its mechanisms evoke a sense of mystery and depth, further complicating the distinction between human and machine.

This interplay is also reflected in the poem's narrative structure, which shifts between the speaker's internal reflections and their sensory engagement with the car. The line *"When was I last with you in this car, / in this closed space?"* (lines 11-12) highlights the car as a site of emotional intimacy and introspection, further dissolving the boundary between the human self and the technological other. The "closed space" of the car becomes a metaphor for the entangled nature of human and machine, encapsulating Braidotti's vision of posthuman subjectivity as fluid and relational.

Building on the themes of relational ontology and vital materiality, the poem also explores how posthuman subjectivity challenges traditional notions of temporality and memory. Braidotti emphasizes the importance of "becoming," a process-oriented approach that focuses on fluidity and transformation rather than static identities. In the poem, the speaker's reflections on the past are filtered through their interactions with the car and its environment, suggesting that memory is not a purely human faculty but one shaped by material entanglements.

The line "A point glows / like an ache for the past" (lines 9-10) encapsulates this idea, portraying memory as a sensory and material phenomenon. The "glow" of the cigarette and the "sharp, bitter aura of petrol" evoke a visceral connection to the past, highlighting how non-human elements mediate the speaker's recollection of previous experiences. This perspective aligns with Braidotti's assertion that subjectivity is not rooted in static notions of selfhood but is continually shaped by interactions with the material world.

Braidotti's theory also carries significant ethical implications, emphasizing the need to reconsider human responsibility in light of our interconnectedness with the non-human. In "Going For A Drive," this ethical dimension is subtly woven into the imagery of industrial decay and environmental degradation. *The "ruined despondent engines" and "bleary pools in dumps"* (lines 21-22) evoke a sense of loss and decay, highlighting the impact of human activity on the environment. However, the poem does not present these elements as mere symbols of destruction. Instead, they are imbued with vitality and beauty, as seen in the "rainbows in their eyes" (line 24), suggesting a need to reevaluate our relationship with the non-human world.

This ethical reconsideration aligns with Braidotti's call for a posthuman ethics that acknowledges the agency of non-human entities and the interconnectedness of all forms of life. By portraying the car and its components as active participants in the speaker's experience, the poem invites readers to reflect on their own entanglements with technology and the environment, challenging anthropocentric notions of control and domination.

Through the perspective of Rosi Braidotti's theory of posthuman subjectivity, "Going For A Drive" emerges as a profound exploration of the entangled relationships between humans, machines, and the environment. The poem's vivid imagery and reflective tone illustrate the fluid boundaries between human and non-human, challenging traditional notions of subjectivity and agency. By emphasizing relational ontology, vital materiality, and the ethical implications of posthumanism, the poem invites readers to reconsider their place in a world where humans and non-humans are inextricably connected. In doing so, it not only reflects the core tenets of Braidotti's posthumanism but also offers a poignant meditation on the complexities of living in a technologically mediated world.

Works Cited

Braidotti, Rosi. "Affirmative Ethics, Posthuman Subjectivity, and Intimate Scholarship: a Conversation with RosiBraidotti." *Decentering the Researcher in Intimate Scholarship*, edited by Emerald Publishing Limited, vol. 31 of Advances in Research on Teaching, Emerald Publishing, 2018, pp. 179–188. DOI: https://doi.org/10.1108/S1479-368720180000031014.

---. *The Posthuman*. Polity, 2013.

Chaudhuri, Amit. *St. Cyril Road and Other Poems*. Penguin Books India, 2005.

Haynes, Patrice. "Creative Becoming and the Patiency of Matter." *Angelaki: Journal of Theoretical Humanities*, vol. 19, no. 1, 2014, pp. 19–27. Taylor and Francis Online, https://doi.org/10.1080/0969725X.2014.920633.

Toffoletti, Kim. "The Posthuman." *Australian Feminist Studies*, vol. 30, no. 84, 2015, pp. 211–213. Taylor and Francis Online, https://doi.org/10.1080/08164649.2015.1038119.

Navigating Hybridity in Temsula Ao's *The Tombstone in My Garden*

Dr K. Anuradha

Associate Professor, PG & Research Department of English,

Government Arts College (Autonomous), Coimbatore.

Temsula Ao's collection, The Tombstone in My Garden, delves into the complexities of identity, cultural displacement, and the lingering effects of colonialism in Naga society. This is evident in the interview "Carving a Niche: An Interview with TemsulaAo," Ao discusses the significance of oral storytelling traditions in preserving the history and culture of communities that have evolved without written records (Longkumer 3). Applying Homi K. Bhabha's postcolonial theory of hybridity illuminates how Ao's characters navigate the "in-between" spaces of cultural interaction, revealing the nuanced and often painful processes of identity formation in a postcolonial context.

Homi K. Bhabha introduces the concept of hybridity to describe the creation of new cultural forms resulting from the interaction between colonizers and the colonized. This process gives rise to a "Third Space," a liminal area where traditional binaries are disrupted, allowing for the emergence of complex identities that transcend simplistic categorizations (Bhabha 37). In this space, individuals negotiate and renegotiate their identities, leading to both opportunities and challenges in self-definition.

The titular story, "The Tombstone in My Garden," exemplifies the struggles of hybrid identity through the character of Lily Anne, the daughter of an English tea planter and a local woman. Lily Anne's mixed heritage places her in a precarious position within both colonial and indigenous societies, leading to experiences of marginalization and identity conflict. Her father's insistence on arranging her marriage to an Anglo-Indian man further complicates her sense of self, as she is coerced into conforming to societal expectations that neither fully accept nor understand her hybrid identity.Lily Anne's internal conflict is evident in her reaction to her husband's death and the presence of his tombstone in her garden. The tombstone symbolizes the oppressive weight of imposed identities and the lingering influence of colonial structures on her personal life. Her decision to remove and relocate the tombstone signifies a rejection of these imposed identities and an attempt to reclaim her sense of self within the "Third Space" of hybridity.

In the short story, "The Platform," Ao explores themes of cultural displacement and the fragility of human bonds through the story of Nandu, a Bihari porter in Dimapur, who adopts an abandoned boy. Upon discovering that the boy is circumcised, indicating his Muslim identity, Nandu fears societal backlash and conceals this information. The boy's eventual exposure and subsequent lynching by the community highlight the deep-seated prejudices and cultural tensions present in postcolonial society.Nandu's experience reflects the challenges of navigating hybrid identities in a society resistant to cultural integration. His initial act of adopting the boy demonstrates an embrace of hybridity, but the violent rejection by the community underscores the dangers and difficulties inherent in occupying the "Third Space." This narrative illustrates Bhabha's assertion that hybridity is fraught with ambivalence, as it simultaneously offers possibilities for new identities and poses threats to established cultural norms (Bhabha 112).

"The Saga of a Cloth," another story in the collection, tells the story of Repasongla, a woman who marries her rapist, Lolen, as part of a long-term plan for revenge. Her act of placing the tassel of her supeti (funeral cloth) on her husband's chest before burial is a profound statement of resistance against the patriarchal and oppressive structures that have governed her life. This act challenges traditional gender roles and societal expectations, creating a space for Repasongla to assert her agency within a restrictive cultural framework.Repasongla's story exemplifies the negotiation of identity within the "Third Space," where she subverts traditional norms to reclaim her sense of self. Her actions reflect the complexities of hybridity, as she navigates the intersections of personal trauma, cultural expectations, and the desire for autonomy. This narrative aligns with Bhabha's concept of mimicry, where the colonized subject imitates the colonizer's behavior, but with a difference that undermines the authority of the colonizer (Bhabha 86).

Ao's stories "Snow-Green" and "The Talking Tree" extend the concept of hybridity to the natural world, portraying plants as sentient beings capable of resistance against human exploitation. In "Snow-Green," a lily refuses to bloom after being transplanted from the open garden to an ornate pot, symbolizing the disruption of natural harmony through human intervention. Similarly, "The Talking Tree" depicts a rebellion by the plant world against human loggers, highlighting the consequences of environmental degradation.These narratives suggest a parallel between cultural and environmental hybridity, emphasizing the interconnectedness of human and natural worlds. The resistance of the plants mirrors the struggles of Ao's human characters, reinforcing the themes of displacement and the search for identity within the "Third Space." This perspective aligns with Bhabha's idea that hybridity is not limited to human cultures but can also encompass the relationships between humans and their environments (Bhabha 219).

TemsulaAo's The Tombstone in My Garden offers a profound exploration of hybridity and the complexities of identity in postcolonial Naga society. Through her nuanced characters and narratives, Ao illustrates the challenges and possibilities inherent in navigating the "Third Space" of cultural interaction. Applying Homi K. Bhabha's theory of hybridity to these stories reveals the intricate processes of identity formation and resistance in the face of colonial legacies and societal expectations. Ao's work underscores the importance of embracing hybridity as a means of understanding and negotiating the multifaceted realities of postcolonial existence.

Works Cited

Ao, Temsula. The Tombstone in My Garden. Speaking Tiger Books, 2022.

Bhabha, Homi K. The Location of Culture. Routledge, 1994.

"Five Stories of TemsulaAo's 'The Tombstone in My Garden' Tell of a Loss of Lost Purpose in Naga Society." Imphal Reviews, 4 June 2022, https://imphalreviews.in/f

Longkumer, I Watitula. "Carving a Niche: An Interview with TemsulaAo." Postcolonial Text, vol. 19, no. 1 & 2, 2024, pp. 1-12.

Analyzing Agastya Sen in Upamanyu Chatterjee's *English, August* through Jungian Concepts of Persona and Shadow

Dr Geetha K. Swamy

Assistant Professor, PG & Research Department of English,

Government Arts College (Autonomous), Coimbatore.

Upamanyu Chatterjee, a former Indian Administrative Service (IAS) officer, burst onto the literary scene with his debut novel, *English, August*: An Indian Story (1988). Often regarded as a modern classic in Indian English literature, the novel blends humor and existential musings to portray the struggles of Agastya Sen, a young urban man thrust into the bureaucratic monotony of rural India. The story, infused with irony and wit, explores identity, disillusionment, and cultural displacement in a rapidly changing India. Agastya, nicknamed "August," oscillates between his urbane upbringing and the stark realities of the provincial town of Madna. This essay applies Carl Jung's concepts of the persona and the shadow to analyze Agastya's personality, providing a deeper understanding of his internal conflicts.

At its core, *English, August* is a coming-of-age story that highlights the conflict between societal expectations and personal desires. By examining Agastya's persona and shadow, we aim to uncover the psychological layers of his character, demonstrating how these Jungian concepts elucidate his alienation, existential struggles, and eventual acceptance of his circumstances.

According to Carl Jung, the persona is the outward identity or "mask" one presents to the world to conform to societal expectations. Jung writes, "The persona is that which in reality one is not, but which oneself as well as others think one is" (Jung 305). In *English, August,* Agastya's persona is shaped by his position as an IAS officer, a prestigious role in Indian society. However, this mask feels alien to him. Early in the novel, his friend Dhrubo observes, *"I've a feeling, August, you're going to get hazaar fucked in Madna"* (Chatterjee 6), signaling Agastya's ill-fit for the rigid expectations of bureaucracy.

Agastya himself is acutely aware of this dissonance. Upon arriving in Madna, he notes, *"What am I doing here? I should have been a photographer, or a maker of ad films, something like that, shallow and urban"* (Chatterjee 50). This acknowledgment reveals his struggle to reconcile his authentic self with the persona demanded by his role. The persona's fragility is further evident in his interactions with colleagues, where he fabricates lies about his marital status and background to maintain a superficial semblance of normalcy. For instance, he claims, *"She's in England. She's English, anyway, but she's gone there for a cancer operation"* (Chatterjee 52), underscoring his discomfort with the personal scrutiny his position entails.

The shadow, as described by Jung, represents the repressed, darker aspects of the psyche—qualities one denies or hides due to societal or personal rejection. Jung posits, "Everyone carries a shadow, and the less it is embodied in the individual's conscious life, the blacker and denser it is" (Jung 91). For Agastya, the shadow manifests through his hedonistic tendencies and deep-seated disillusionment.

Agastya's marijuana use and sexual fantasies serve as outlets for his shadow. These acts, which starkly contrast with the decorum expected of an IAS officer, signify his rebellion against the constraints of his persona. Reflecting on his routine, he muses, *"Should I smoke a joint? After all, the jeep wouldn't come till eleven. While wondering, he made one and smoked it anyway"* (Chatterjee 60). This casual indulgence highlights his escapism and the shadow's influence on his actions.Moreover, Agastya's existential musings are tinged with cynicism, further exposing his shadow. Observing the stagnation and hypocrisy in Madna, he remarks, *"The world outside is not worth journeying out for"* (Chatterjee 75). This pessimism aligns with Jung's assertion that confronting the shadow involves facing uncomfortable truths about oneself and the world. Agastya's sense of alienation, his disdain for bureaucratic rituals, and his fantasies about a different life underscore the shadow's hold over his psyche.

Agastya's journey in *English, August* is marked by a tension between his persona and shadow. While his persona demands adherence to societal norms, his shadow urges him to reject these constraints and embrace his true desires. This internal conflict often leaves him paralyzed, unable to fully commit to either path.For instance, Agastya's persona requires him to navigate the formalities of rural administration, yet his shadow finds these duties absurd. During an inspection of a village well, he observes the *"muteness of the village" and the grim reality of children scouring the well for water, likening it to "some mythic punishment"* (Chatterjee 105). His empathy and horror clash with his inability to enact meaningful change, reflecting his deeper struggle with authenticity and responsibility.

Agastya's humor and self-deprecation also reflect this conflict. By mocking his own role, he attempts to bridge the gap between his persona and shadow. When a colleague comments on his unsuitability for the IAS, he quips, *"I'd much rather act in a porn film than be a bureaucrat. But I suppose one has to live"* (Chatterjee 12). Such moments reveal his awareness of the charade he perpetuates, even as he feels trapped by it.

Jung argues that individuation—the process of integrating the persona, shadow, and other archetypes—is essential for personal growth. He writes, *"One does not become enlightened by imagining figures of light, but by making the darkness conscious"* (Jung 265). By the novel's conclusion, Agastya exhibits signs of this integration. Though he does not undergo a dramatic transformation, he begins to accept the necessity of his circumstances without entirely relinquishing his individuality.

The turning point comes when Agastya reflects on a colleague's rudimentary painting in the Rest House. Initially dismissive, he later recognizes the humanity and effort behind it, thinking, *"This was the Goa of an imagination forlorn, not accustomed to creativity, but compelled to it by isolation"* (Chatterjee 95). This moment of empathy indicates his growing ability to reconcile the disparate parts of his psyche, embracing both the mundane and the profound.

In *English, August*, Upamanyu Chatterjee masterfully portrays the internal struggles of Agastya Sen through the lens of Jungian psychology. The tension between Agastya's persona and shadow encapsulates his alienation and search for meaning in a world that often feels absurd. By examining these conflicts, we gain insight into his journey toward self-awareness and acceptance. As Agastya navigates the labyrinth of rural bureaucracy and personal discontent, he offers a poignant reminder of the complexities of identity and the human condition.

Works Cited

Chatterjee, Upamanyu. *English, August*: An Indian Story. Faber and Faber, 1988.

Jung, Carl G. The Archetypes and the Collective Unconscious. Translated by R.F.C. Hull, Princeton University Press, 1981.

The Unquiet Woods and Deep Ecology: An Examination

Dr G. Subramanian

Assistant Professor, Post Graduate & Research Department of English

Government Arts College (Autonomous), Coimbatore

Deep Ecology, a theory articulated by Norwegian philosopher Arne Naess, emphasizes the intrinsic value of all living beings and ecosystems, challenging the anthropocentric worldview that treats nature as a mere resource for human consumption. In Ramachandra Guha's The Unquiet Woods: Ecological Change and Peasant Resistance in the Himalaya, this framework proves particularly apt for exploring the book's themes of environmental degradation, peasant resistance, and colonial exploitation. Guha's analysis of the Chipko movement and the broader ecological history of the Indian Himalaya resonates deeply with Deep Ecology's principles, as it critiques reductionist, human-centered approaches to nature while championing a harmonious coexistence rooted in traditional knowledge systems.

Deep Ecology posits that nature possesses intrinsic value beyond its utility to humans. Naess emphasizes, "The flourishing of human and non-human life on Earth has value in itself" (Naess 28). Guha's work echoes this principle through his portrayal of Himalayan forests as integral to the ecological and cultural fabric of Uttarakhand. For instance, he writes, *"The forests were not merely a source of fuel and fodder but formed the very basis of the peasantry's subsistence economy"* (Guha 55). This statement underscores how these forests are vital not only for human survival but also for maintaining ecological balance.

Guha's critique of colonial forestry practices highlights the violation of Deep Ecology's tenets. Under British rule, forests were commodified and exploited for timber and revenue, alienating local communities from their traditional stewardship roles. He notes, *"Colonial forestry policies undermined the intricate linkages between forests and subsistence agriculture, leading to ecological degradation and social discontent"* (Guha 63). This commodification directly opposes the biocentric equality at the heart of Deep Ecology, which views all living entities as equal participants in Earth's ecological web.

The Chipko movement, central to Guha's narrative, embodies Deep Ecology's resistance to anthropocentric exploitation. The movement's iconic practice of hugging trees to prevent logging illustrates a profound respect for nature's inherent value. Guha writes, *"The peasants' resistance was less about opposing modernization per se and more about defending their traditional rights over forests that sustained their way of life"* (Guha 172). Here, the Chipko activists reject the utilitarian mindset that prioritizes economic growth over ecological integrity.

Scholarly commentary further substantiates this perspective. Vandana Shiva argues that Chipko was not merely an environmental movement but *"a social philosophy that challenges the patriarchal and capitalist exploitation of nature"* (Shiva 42). This analysis aligns with Deep Ecology's call for a radical shift in values—from domination to partnership with the natural world.

Deep Ecology emphasizes the interconnectedness of all life forms, rejecting hierarchical structures that place humans above nature. Guha illustrates this principle by exploring how deforestation disrupts the intricate balance between forests, agriculture, and local communities. He observes, *"Deforestation triggered soil erosion, reduced agricultural productivity, and increased the frequency of natural disasters, underscoring the ecological interdependence of Himalayan life systems"* (Guha 144).

Traditional knowledge systems, as highlighted in The Unquiet Woods, reflect a deep understanding of this interconnectedness. Guha writes about the indigenous management of forests: *"Local communities adhered to practices that ensured sustainable use, such as rotational grazing and selective felling, which maintained the ecological equilibrium"* (Guha 28). These practices resonate with Deep Ecology's emphasis on respecting ecological limits and prioritizing the long-term health of ecosystems over short-term gains.

Guha's critique of colonial forestry policies aligns closely with Deep Ecology's opposition to reductionist, technocratic approaches to nature. He argues that British forestry practices were rooted in an exploitative ethos that ignored the cultural and ecological significance of forests. *"The colonial state's vision of scientific forestry prioritized revenue generation over ecological stability, transforming forests into mere economic assets"* (Guha 59). This perspective is supported by MadhavGadgil and Ramachandra Guha in their joint work, This Fissured Land, where they state, *"The colonial model of resource extraction disrupted traditional systems of ecological management, creating enduring social and environmental conflicts"* (Gadgil and Guha 112).

Deep Ecology challenges such reductionism by advocating for holistic, ecosystem-based approaches. Naess contends, *"Ecological science itself teaches that the boundaries of ecosystems — and the relationships within them — cannot be understood in isolation"* (Naess 45). The colonial focus on maximizing timber yields disregarded this holistic understanding, leading to widespread ecological degradation and social unrest.

The Chipko movement's prominent inclusion of women activists underscores Deep Ecology's principle of egalitarianism across all forms of life. Guha highlights the crucial role of women in resisting deforestation: *"Women, who bore the brunt of ecological degradation through increased labor and reduced subsistence resources, emerged as key leaders in the Chipko movement"* (Guha 165). Their activism reflects a deep ecological consciousness rooted in lived experience and communal knowledge.

Ecofeminist scholars like Ariel Salleh have drawn connections between Deep Ecology and feminist critiques of environmental exploitation. Salleh argues, *"Women's ecological knowledge, derived from their roles as caregivers and sustainers of life, offers invaluable insights into sustainable practices"* (Salleh 83). The Chipko women's leadership exemplifies this synergy, demonstrating how marginalized voices can lead the way toward ecological harmony.

One of Deep Ecology's core tenets is the rejection of anthropocentrism in favor of ecocentrism. The Chipko movement's success in halting deforestation serves as a powerful case study of how grassroots resistance can challenge dominant paradigms. Guha writes, *"Chipko's moral philosophy, rooted in Gandhian principles of nonviolence and ecological justice, offered a compelling alternative to the exploitative ethos of modern forestry"* (Guha 178).

This shift from exploitation to stewardship aligns with Naess's vision of an ecological society. He writes, *"A deep ecological attitude seeks not to conquer nature but to coexist with it, recognizing our interdependence with the natural world"* (Naess 36). By framing forests as commons rather than commodities, the Chipko movement embodies this ethos and challenges the dominant logic of resource extraction.

Analyzing The Unquiet Woods through the lens of Deep Ecology reveals the text's profound engagement with ecological philosophy and its critique of exploitative environmental practices. Guha's work highlights the interconnectedness of social and ecological systems, the intrinsic value of nature, and the need for sustainable, community-driven approaches to resource management. The Chipko movement, as portrayed in the book, serves as a model for resisting anthropocentric exploitation and embracing a more harmonious relationship with nature.

In a world increasingly grappling with the consequences of environmental degradation, Guha's insights and the principles of Deep Ecology offer invaluable lessons. They challenge us to rethink our relationship with the natural world and to prioritize ecological integrity over short-term economic gains, ensuring a sustainable future for all life forms.

Works Cited

Gadgil, Madhav, and Ramachandra Guha. This Fissured Land: An Ecological History of India. Oxford University Press, 1993.

Guha, Ramachandra. The Unquiet Woods: Ecological Change and Peasant Resistance in the Himalaya. Expanded ed., University of California Press, 2000.

Naess, Arne. Ecology, Community, and Lifestyle: Outline of an Ecosophy. Translated by David Rothenberg, Cambridge University Press, 1989.

Salleh, Ariel. "Ecofeminism as Politics: Nature, Marx, and the Postmodern." Zed Books, 1997.

Shiva, Vandana. Staying Alive: Women, Ecology, and Development. Kali for Women, 1988.

Postmodern Analysis of "Mohandas" by Rajmohan Gandhi

Dr D. Shanthi

Assistant Professor, PG & Research Department of English

Government Arts College (Autonomous), Coimbatore.

Postmodernism, with its focus on deconstruction, fragmentation, and the questioning of universal truths, offers a compelling framework through which to analyze Rajmohan Gandhi's Mohandas: A True Story of a Man, His People, and an Empire. This biography of Mahatma Gandhi explores not only the well-documented political and ethical dimensions of Gandhi's life but also delves into his personal struggles, relationships, and the cultural complexities of colonial India. By applying the postmodern theory of historiography as advocated by Hayden White—who posits that historical narratives are shaped by the subjective choices of their authors—we can critically examine the text's construction of Gandhi's identity and its portrayal of historical events.

One of the hallmarks of postmodern thought is its emphasis on the fragmented and constructed nature of identity. In Mohandas, Gandhi is portrayed not as a monolithic figure but as a man of contradictions and evolving beliefs. For instance, the text reveals Gandhi's early fears, his struggles with lust, and his complex relationship with his wife, Kasturba. These personal dimensions challenge the hagiographic image of Gandhi as a saintly leader.

Gandhi's confession of stealing gold from his brother's armlet and the profound impact of his father's forgiveness exemplify his moral growth. Gandhi writes:

"Pearl-drops trickled down his cheeks, wetting the paper. For a moment he closed his eyes in thought and then tore up the note… Those pearl-drops of love cleansed my heart and washed my sin away." (Mohandas)

This deeply personal moment deconstructs the myth of Gandhi as inherently virtuous, emphasizing instead the gradual and human process of ethical development.

Hayden White's theory suggests that historical narratives are not neutral; they are shaped by the author's interpretative choices, including their selection of events and the narrative structure they employ. Rajmohan Gandhi acknowledges this subjectivity in the preface:

"This study is a bid to free Gandhi the person from his image or images, and to present his life fully and honestly." (Mohandas)

Despite this aim, the biography's portrayal of Gandhi as a "discoverer of satyagraha" and a "pioneer of religious pluralism" reflects the author's admiration. This inherent bias aligns with White's argument that the construction of historical figures is inevitably influenced by the author's perspective. The narrative oscillates between portraying Gandhi as a hero and as a flawed individual, creating a complex tapestry that resists simplistic categorization.

Postmodernism often interrogates power dynamics and the grand narratives that sustain them. Mohandas challenges the colonial narrative of British benevolence by highlighting the systemic racism and economic exploitation inherent in colonial rule. The book recounts Gandhi's experience of racial discrimination in South Africa, where he was thrown off a train for refusing to vacate a first-class compartment. This pivotal incident is described with stark simplicity:

"He was ordered to leave the compartment… When he refused, he was forcibly ejected and his luggage flung out after him." (Mohandas)

By juxtaposing such personal humiliations with Gandhi's eventual leadership in anti-colonial movements, the text deconstructs the colonial narrative of civility and progress, revealing its violent underpinnings.

Postmodern theory also critiques the idea of homogeneous national identities. Mohandas reveals the fractures within Indian society, including caste hierarchies, religious tensions, and gender inequalities. For example, Gandhi's early interactions with the "untouchable" boy Uka highlight the entrenched caste prejudices of his time:

"Putlibai told her children that they were not to touch Uka… Mohan had 'tussles' with her on the question and smiled at her reasoning, yet he tried to obey the injunction." (Mohandas)

This anecdote underscores the complexities of Gandhi's reformist agenda, which sought to bridge societal divisions while grappling with his own ingrained biases. Such moments illustrate the fragmented and contested nature of Indian identity, challenging the notion of a unified nationalist movement.

The biography's narrative style alternates between detailed historical analysis and personal anecdotes, reflecting a postmodern skepticism of linear and objective storytelling. Rajmohan Gandhi's use of direct quotes from Gandhi's writings and speeches adds layers of authenticity while simultaneously reminding readers of the mediated nature of historical knowledge. For instance, the text quotes Gandhi's reflections on truth:

"The little fleeting glimpses... have given me great joy. They have lightened my path and filled me with a certainty of hope." (Mohandas)

These introspective passages emphasize Gandhi's subjective experience, inviting readers to question the reliability of any singular narrative about his life.

Postmodernism often challenges the Enlightenment ideals of rationality and progress. Gandhi's own critique of modern civilization, articulated in Hind Swaraj and echoed in Mohandas, aligns with this scepticism. He questioned the industrialization and materialism of Western modernity, advocating instead for a return to simple living and spiritual values. This critique is summarized in the book:

"For Gandhi, true progress lay in the moral and spiritual awakening of individuals and communities, not in technological advancements." (Mohandas)

Scholars have examined Gandhi's critique of modern civilization through a postmodern lens. One analysis notes, "Gandhi challenged the idea of progress as presented in modern civilization, calling for a return to more natural values and ways of life, which he claimed would be more sustainable and harmonious" ("Mahatma Gandhi"). This perspective aligns with postmodern scepticism toward grand narratives of progress.

This perspective challenges the dominant narrative of colonial modernity as a civilizing force, positioning Gandhi as a dissenting voice against the homogenizing tendencies of globalization.

Gandhi's opposition to industrialization and materialism reflects a postmodern critique of modernity. He *"rejected modern civilization and opposed Nehru's concept and approach to development,"* (Sahu & Sarangi) advocating instead for decentralized, village-based economies. This stance questions the universal desirability of Western models of progress.

Postmodern texts often employ intertextuality, drawing connections between different works and cultural contexts. Mohandas references Gandhi's autobiography, The Story of My Experiments with Truth, as well as historical documents and accounts from contemporaries. These intertextual elements enrich the narrative while highlighting the multiplicity of perspectives surrounding Gandhi's life. For instance, Rajmohan Gandhi contrasts Gandhi's philosophy of nonviolence with the violent realities of the Partition, creating a dialogue between ideals and historical contingencies.

The applicability of Gandhi's ideas in contemporary postmodern contexts has been explored, suggesting that "the perspective of Gandhi is more relevant in the postmodern era" (Rudolph). This relevance is attributed to his emphasis on localism, nonviolence, and ethical living, which resonate with postmodern values.

Applying postmodern theory to Mohandas reveals the layered and constructed nature of Rajmohan Gandhi's narrative. By deconstructing Gandhi's identity, interrogating colonial and nationalist discourses, and embracing narrative multiplicity, the biography resists reductive interpretations of its subject. It invites readers to grapple with the complexities of Gandhi's life and legacy, offering a nuanced portrayal that aligns with postmodernism's commitment to plurality and skepticism of grand narratives. As Hayden White suggests, history is as much a product of imagination as it is of evidence, and Mohandas exemplifies this interplay, presenting a Gandhi who is both a product of his time and a transformative force within it.

Works Cited

Gandhi, Rajmohan. Mohandas: A True Story of a Man, his
    People and an Empire. Penguin, 2006.

"Mahatma Gandhi: Readings in a Postmodern Light."
    MKGandhi.org,
    https://www.mkgandhi.org/articles/ Mahatma-
    Gandhi-readings-in-a-postmodern-light.php.
    Accessed 15 Jan. 2025.

"Post-Modernist Gandhi: A Study of Gandhism and
    Gandhigiri and People's Perceptions." ResearchGate,
    https://www.researchgate.net/publication/3675197
    49_Post-
    Modernist_Gandhi_A_Study_of_Gandhism_and_
    Gandhigiri_and_People%27s_Perceptions. Accessed
    15 Jan. 2025.

Rudolph, Lloyd I. "Postmodern Gandhi." Postmodern
    Gandhi and Other Essays: Gandhi in the World and
    at Home, University of Chicago Press, 2006, pp. 3-59.
    https://www.degruyter.com/document/doi/10.720
    8/9780226731315-002/pdf. Accessed 15 Jan. 2025.

Sahu, Sanjaya, and Harihar Sarangi. "Postmodern Gandhi:
    A Light Bearer of 21st Century." International
    Journal of Advanced Academic Studies, vol. 3, no. 3,
    2021, pp. 1-5.
    https://www.allstudyjournal.com/article/561/3-2-
    32-876.pdf. Accessed 15 Jan. 2025.

Postcritiquing Jeet Thayil's "The Haunts" - An Appreciation

Dr G. Karthikeyani

Assistant Professor, PG & Research Department of English

Government Arts College (Autonomous), Coimbatore

Jeet Thayil's poem "The Haunts" is a rich exploration of memory, loss, and existential reflections. To analyze this poem, we apply the principles of postcritique, a 21st-century literary theory championed by Rita Felski, which emphasizes moving beyond traditional critical approaches to explore literature in ways that combine analysis with emotional attachment. Felski's postcritique invites readers to engage with texts affectively, examining their ability to evoke feelings and foster connections rather than solely dissecting their meaning ("Postcritique").

Thayil's use of vivid, layered imagery creates a sensory-rich experience, inviting readers to confront emotions evoked by transience and decay. The opening lines establish a tone of ethereal ambiguity:

"As starlight, as ash or rain, as a smear on the moon," (Thayil)

These comparisons blend the celestial and the earthly, highlighting the fleeting and fragile nature of existence (Thayil 1). According to Felski, literature acts as *"an exercise in aesthetic re-education,"* prompting readers to reassess their perceptions and emotions (Felski, The Limits of Critique). Thayil's imagery achieves this by juxtaposing beauty with ephemerality, drawing readers into a state of introspection.

As the poem progresses, the imagery becomes increasingly visceral, as seen in the line:

"as the smell of a small dead animal," (Thayil)

This description engages the reader's senses directly, fostering an intimate and unsettling connection to the text (Thayil 5). Postcritique emphasizes such affective engagements, where readers experience the text's emotional power alongside its intellectual implications (Felski, The Uses of Literature).

The poem's repetitive structure, characterized by its use of "as" clauses, creates a hypnotic rhythm. This incantatory quality mirrors the persistence of haunting memories, drawing the reader into the cyclical nature of trauma and reflection:

"as the stalker at 4 AM swing creaking in the park near my house downturned face white in cellphone light," (Thayil)

This structure evokes a sense of inevitability, as though each image emerges unbidden from the recesses of memory (Thayil 16). Postcritique encourages readers to appreciate the interplay between form and content, recognizing how structure contributes to a text's emotional and aesthetic resonance ("Postcritique").

Isolation is a central theme in "The Haunts", portrayed through solitary figures and introspective moments. The lines *"as a figure by the side of the Expressway urging me to crash the car in a voice so calm and wise it took every shred of sanity not to give in,"* depict a chilling encounter with internalized despair (Thayil 25). Such imagery reflects the urban alienation often explored in Thayil's work. A review in The Caravan notes that his poetry frequently grapples with themes of estrangement and isolation, drawing from his personal experiences ("Sorrow and Sensibility").

The poem also delves into existential questions, contemplating life, death, and the afterlife. The lines:

"as the abandoned child you werewho said goodbye to wind and waterstepped into the opposite of airsaid no to earthblood," (Thayil evoke a journey beyond the physical realm, prompting reflections on mortality and spiritual transcendence (Thayil 42). Postcritique encourages such reflections, allowing readers to explore philosophical insights gleaned through the act of reading (Felski, The Limits of Critique).

Thayil's personal history with addiction and his experiences in various cities inform much of the imagery in "The Haunts". The reference to "bad heroin in a Delhi alley" draws from his lived experiences, adding authenticity to his portrayal of urban despair (Thayil 19). An interview in The Guardian highlights how Thayil's years as a drug addict in Mumbai and New York deeply influence his work ("JeetThayil: 'I Have a Liver Condition'").

By acknowledging the interplay between the poet's life and his literary output, readers can engage with the text on a more intimate level, appreciating the nuances that personal experience brings to literary expression. Postcritique aligns with this perspective, valuing the connections between the author's context and the text ("Postcritique").

Applying a postcritical lens to Jeet Thayil's"The Haunts" allows readers to engage with the poem's emotional depth, vivid imagery, and existential themes in a holistic manner. By moving beyond traditional critical methods and embracing an approach that combines analysis with attachment, we can fully appreciate the affective power of Thayil's poetry and the rich tapestry of experiences it conveys.

Works Cited

Felski, Rita. The Limits of Critique. University of Chicago Press, 2015.

---. The Uses of Literature. Blackwell Publishing, 2008.

"Jeet Thayil: 'I Have a Liver Condition, I'm Reckless and I'm Very Aware …'" The Guardian, 9 Feb. 2018, https://www.theguardian.com/books/2018/feb/09/jeet-thayil-interview-man-booker-narcopolis-book-chocolate-saints.

Mehrotra, Palash Krishna. "Sorrow and Sensibility in the Poetry of Jeet Thayil." The Caravan, 1 Aug. 2016, https://caravanmagazine.in/reviews-essays/if-there-is-such-a-thing-as-happiness.

"Postcritique." Wikipedia, https://en.wikipedia.org/wiki/Postcritique.

Thayil, Jeet. "The Haunts". Collected Poems, Aleph Book Company, 2015.

A Critical Analysis of Literary Heritage towards Wisdom, Knowledge and Empowerment among Readers

Dr. R. Sumathi
Assistant Professor, Department of English (Aided),
Kongunadu Arts & Science College (Autonomous), Coimbatore

Dr. P. Sujatha
Assistant Professor, Department of English (Aided),
Kongunadu Arts & Science College (Autonomous), Coimbatore

Ms. G. Priya
Ph.D Scholar, Department of English (Aided),
Kongunadu Arts & Science College (Autonomous), Coimbatore

Luck may bring you riches, but it will never bring you wisdom.

Indian writers such as Ruskin Bond, R.K. Narayan and Anuradha Roy who are all have acquired English as a second language, are taking the Culture and Tradition of India to adjacent decade. Ruskin Bond is the first-generation British migrant, one who considers himself as a 'Visual Writer' as he was very fond of writing his favourite genres of Essays and Short stories and he is a well renowned person one who inspires Indian Readers and writers. Bond inspires the readers as he received his award John Llewellyn Rhys for his work Room on the Roof and later received Sahitya Academy Award in 1992 for 'Our Trees Still Grow in Dehra' a collection of Autobiographical about the town Dehradun in India. Subsequently, on the other hand the Indian epic writer of 20th Century R.K. Narayan, the most admired author of Hindu tradition and culture stir up the rising generation and guide them into spiritual strength through his novel the guide and describes the transformation of the hero of the novel Raju (the name which he uses very often on his novels for the protagonist) and there he is called as one the greatest holy men of India whereas the work earned him the first 1960 Sahitya Academy Award for English and it was included on the Big Jubilee Read list of 70 book by commonwealth authors selected to celebrate the platinum jubilee of Elizabeth. The other privileged Indian author Anuradha Roy who received the prestigious Sahitya Academy Award 2022 which was announced for 23 languages on December 22, 2022 for her novel "All the Lives We Never Lived' which was published in the year of 2018 and also was shortlisted for the International Dublin Literary Awards. 'In her novel she portrayed about a family who were struggling by unpredictable ways to encourage nationalism and an enormous transformations among the readers and future generation.

RUSKIN BOND'S CHILDHOOD WITH NATURE TO DELINEATE THE IMPORTANCE OF RELATIONSHIP:

The responsibility of every generation depends upon how they lead their own relationship with their relatives, friends and with the strangers they meet in their day to day life. Naturally it leads to a healthy and active motivation among youngsters toward wisdom, harmony and peace of India to the direction of tradition and culture. Ceaselessly the same has been exposed in Ruskin Bond's collection of autobiographical stories captures his childhood, describes the deep attachment of his own town and its surroundings of nature in his award winning novel 'Our trees still grow in Dehra'. Most of his stories including his childhood were written in Maplewood. He felt that the old cottage was kind to a struggling young writer. Even if he knew that the cottage has disappeared, he moved to write, enjoyed writing on the picturesque of woodwork, jungle, leaves, the butterfly tree, the very tall cottage, woodpeckers, insects, a steep path, and heavy rain in Dehradun. To make his dream come true he struggled in his young age and in his age of thirty five he decided to take a few risks. So he felt it was the right time to do something about it. In his novel he has given a note on 'Escape form Java', it was the time of World War II. He Spent his time with his new companion Sono (who was about his age and could speak in English), son of a college professor who could speak Dutch, Chinese, Javanese and a little English. They enjoyed together with the pastime that they spent on flying kite in the park. Since, he is called as a virtual writer his rusty stories have been adapted into doordharshan tv series Ek Tha Rusty. Including the night train at Deoli, Time stops at Shamli and Our Trees still grow in Dehra have been incorporated into the school curriculum in India. Recently, he made his maiden big-screen appearance with an Vishal Bharadwaj's film 7 Khoon Maaf in 2011, based on his short story Sussanna's seven husbands. Bond appears as a bishop in the movie with actress Priyanka Chopra playing the title role. Bond had earlier collaborated with Bharadwaj in the Blue Umbrella which was based one of his works.

INNOVATION AND INSPIRATION OF NARAYAN'S NOVEL 'THE GUIDE':

One could be surprised to hear an Indo - Anglian was never a good student. Narayan failed both in school and intermediate examinations. He might be able to get his degree only at his age of Twenty – five. His personality was affected as a result of these failures when he studied. As he failed at school and college he lost confidence, became shy and reserved. After completed his graduation from Maharaja College, he joined in Mysore Secretariat as a clerk to support his family financially. Later he devoted his time to writing even he got opportunity to work as a school teacher. Narayan was recognized as genius writer when he was awarded the Sahitya Academy Award in 1960 for his work 'The Guide'. He is very famous and popular not only in India but also in Europe and America for he has been added in the list of writers and their works being published by the British Council. One of the most popular novels of R.K. Narayan is 'The Guide'. In a very short time the novel got great attention of the readers and it was translated into many languages. It narrates the protagonist named Railway Raju a well known tourist guide, turned prisoner and the prisoner turned swami, later becomes a martyr for the cause of the common people. The novel explains how deviation from tradition leads to chaos and conformity to tradition leads to order and happiness. Through self – sacrifice man aspires for greatness and achieves salvation towards empowerment. R.K. Narayan's the guide on wisdom and the will to live; it deliberately portrays how man's absurd attempts to achieve salvation result in his death.

FREEDOM OF KNOWLEDGE LEARNING IN ANURADHA ROY'S SAHITYA ACADEMY WINNING NOVEL:

"Innocents are what make humankind human"

Anuradha Roy depicted her fourth novel 'All the Lives We Never Lived' for the future decade is contending with large themes of freedom nationalism and nature against the turbulent backdrop of India's fight for Independence and World War II, the battle against colonialism and a woman's against marital trap. She completely portrays one family's troubles with desire and loss to the more universal struggles. The way of her storytelling is mesmerizing on the consequences of freedom, love and loyalty is an astonishing display for the writers and readers of literary works. Her novel gives more scope on reading to the readers. This novel of Roy is beautifully written and has described as a gripping story of families fall apart and of what remains in the aftermath.

Therefore the novels Our Trees still grow in Dehra, The Guide, and All Lives that We Never Lived, written by Ruskin Bond, R. K. Narayan and Anuradha Roy those were received Sahitya Academy Awards compiled with the themes of freedom, wisdom, knowledge and empowerment of writers and readers which gives hope with the people to spread harmony among society and into the country on treasuring the tradition and culture of our decade to expand Literary heritage.

"Leave those buds alone. Let the flowers bloom!"

References:

The Guide – R. K. Narayan, Amarjeet S. Chopra, Unique Publishers.

Our Trees Still Grow in Dehra, Bond Ruskin, South and Southeast Asian Literature, Penguin Uk Publisher, 2011.

All the Lives that We Never Lived, Roy Anuradha, Perera – Hussein Publishing House, Colombo – 2018.

Marginalization of the Subaltern Woman: An Analysis of The Walled City by Esther David Through the perspective of Gayatri Chakravorty Spivak's Postcolonial Feminist Theory

Ms A. Dhanuvarcini

Assistant Professor of English

RVS College of Arts & Science, Coimbatore

Gayatri Chakravorty Spivak's postcolonial feminist theory offers an insightful framework for analyzing Esther David's The Walled City (2009), a novel that intricately weaves together themes of displacement, identity, and gender oppression within the Jewish community in postcolonial India. Spivak's seminal essay "Can the Subaltern Speak?" interrogates the silencing of marginalized voices, particularly women, within colonial and postcolonial power structures. By applying Spivak's tenets to The Walled City, this essay explores how Esther David critiques the patriarchal and communal boundaries that render women voiceless, while simultaneously presenting a nuanced portrait of cultural hybridity and agency.

Spivak argues that the subaltern, especially the subaltern woman, is systematically denied a voice within colonial and postcolonial frameworks, as their experiences are mediated and interpreted through dominant discourses (Spivak 66). In The Walled City, the narrator's mother, Naomi, becomes emblematic of this silencing. As a working woman in a patriarchal Jewish household, Naomi is constantly scrutinized and marginalized for transgressing traditional gender roles. The narrator reflects, "True, my mother Naomi does less housework than Aunty Hannah or Granny… The women of the house think that Mother is far too independent and they have always been a little jealous of her" (David 7). Naomi's independence as a wage earner disrupts the established gender dynamics, yet her voice is subsumed by the familial and societal expectations that define women's roles.

Spivak's critique of "textualizing" subaltern women's experiences resonates here. Naomi's struggles are mediated through the narrator's perspective, rendering her voice secondary and framed within the confines of patriarchal interpretation. Her defiance of traditional roles does not translate into liberation but instead isolates her further. Spivak's assertion that the subaltern woman's agency is often co-opted or silenced by the structures she seeks to challenge is evident in Naomi's experience.

A recurring theme in The Walled City is the negotiation of identity within a multicultural and postcolonial context. Spivak's concept of the "epistemic violence" of colonialism—where indigenous cultures and identities are overwritten by colonial discourses—is particularly relevant to the Jewish community's struggle to preserve their traditions in India. The narrator's reflections on her Jewish heritage reveal a deep conflict: *"I look at my image in the mirror. I am but a wisp of that memory… My complexion is a deep brown like Subhadra's and my long plait is tied with red tassels. I could be her sister"* (David 22). Here, the narrator's Indian identity appears to blur the boundaries of her Jewishness, challenging the essentialist notions of cultural purity that Spivak critiques.

Spivak's emphasis on cultural hybridity as a site of both conflict and possibility is crucial in understanding the narrator's journey. The walled city itself becomes a metaphor for the barriers—both physical and cultural—that define and constrain identity. The narrator's struggle to reconcile her Jewish heritage with her Indian upbringing mirrors Spivak's assertion that postcolonial identities are marked by a constant tension between assimilation and resistance (Spivak 73).

Spivak's critique of patriarchal structures that domesticate and discipline women's voices is central to The Walled City. The narrator's childhood is marked by observations of how women are confined within the boundaries of family and tradition. The narrator's friend Subhadra embodies the tragic consequences of this confinement: *"Her mother tells her that she herself was married at five and had never gone to school. Subhadra will be thirteen and at least knows how to read and write"* (David 41). Subhadra's aspirations for education and autonomy are crushed by the expectations of her family, reflecting Spivak's observation that women in traditional societies are often relegated to roles that serve patriarchal interests.

The motif of silencing recurs in Subhadra's fate. When Subhadra's body is discovered in a lily pond, the narrator reflects on the cultural and familial forces that led to her death: *"We are not allowed to talk about Subhadra. Mother does not want me to live in the shadow of death"* (David 43). Subhadra's voice is literally and symbolically erased, reinforcing Spivak's claim that the subaltern woman cannot speak within patriarchal and communal frameworks.

Despite the pervasive structures of silencing, The Walled City also highlights moments of resistance and agency. Spivak's notion of "strategic essentialism"—the temporary adoption of collective identity to resist oppression—is evident in the narrator's attempts to preserve her Jewish heritage. The Shabbat rituals, for instance, become acts of cultural resistance in a rapidly changing world: *"We always look forward to the days when we cover our heads with handkerchiefs and stand, pushing against the table, while Uncle Menachem says the prayers… The words mean nothing to us"* (David 29). While the younger generation may not fully understand the rituals, their participation represents a defiance of cultural erasure.

Similarly, the narrator's reflections on her friendship with Subhadra underscore the importance of cross-cultural solidarity. Despite their differing religious and cultural backgrounds, the two girls forge a bond that challenges the communal divisions around them. This solidarity becomes a subtle form of resistance against the patriarchal and communal forces that seek to confine them.

Through the perspective of Gayatri Chakravorty Spivak's postcolonial feminist theory, The Walled City emerges as a powerful critique of the silencing and marginalization of women within patriarchal and communal structures. Esther David's portrayal of the Jewish community in postcolonial India reflects Spivak's insights into the intersections of gender, culture, and power. By illuminating the struggles and resistances of its female characters, the novel challenges the epistemic violence that renders subaltern women voiceless, while also celebrating the agency and resilience that enable them to navigate and resist these constraints. In doing so, The Walled City not only gives voice to its marginalized characters but also underscores the transformative potential of cross-cultural solidarity and feminist critique.

Works Cited

David, Esther. The Walled City. Westland Ltd, 2009.

Spivak, GayatriChakravorty. "Can the Subaltern Speak?"
    Marxism and the Interpretation of Culture, edited by
    Cary Nelson and Lawrence Grossberg, University of
    Illinois Press, 1988, pp. 66-111.

A Critical Commentary on Arundhati Roy's Essay, "The Algebra of Infinite Justice"

Mr. Parthasarathi A.

Assistant Professor, Department of English,

Bishop Ambrose College, Coimbatore.

Arundhati Roy's essay "The Algebra of Infinite Justice," written in the aftermath of the September 11 attacks, presents a powerful critique of American foreign policy, military interventions, and the rhetoric surrounding the "war on terror." Through a combination of incisive analysis, evocative prose, and sharp irony, Roy challenges the simplistic binaries of good versus evil propagated by the United States government and mainstream media. Her tone is deeply critical, sometimes bordering on the polemical, yet remains anchored in a rich historical and political context. By employing rhetorical strategies such as juxtaposition, irony, and allegory, Roy dismantles the moral justifications for America's retaliatory stance while exposing the historical injustices that contributed to the events of 9/11.

Roy's tone throughout the essay is acerbic, uncompromising, and emotionally charged. She refuses to adopt a detached or neutral stance, instead foregrounding the grief, hypocrisy, and underlying power dynamics that shape global conflicts. Her opening passage, where she critiques the mainstream media's framing of the attacks as a battle between "good and evil," immediately sets the stage for her argument: "Here's the rub: America is at war against people it doesn't know, because they don't appear much on TV" (Roy).

By using the phrase "people it doesn't know," Roy critiques the lack of nuance in American foreign policy, which often operates on reductionist dichotomies. Her use of colloquial phrasing, such as "Here's the rub," lends an immediacy to her argument, making it accessible while maintaining its intellectual depth.

The use of irony is particularly striking in her discussion of the rushed formation of an international coalition against terror. Roy remarks: *"Before it has properly identified or even begun to comprehend the nature of its enemy, the US government has, in a rush of publicity and embarrassing rhetoric, cobbled together an 'international coalition against terror'"* (Roy).

The phrase "embarrassing rhetoric" underscores her skepticism towards the performative nature of American diplomacy, where alliances are hastily formed to serve immediate strategic interests rather than genuine global security.

A major strength of Roy's essay is her ability to interweave historical events into her analysis, thereby exposing the contradictions of American moral authority. She recalls the U.S.'s past interventions in the Middle East and South Asia, particularly its role in Afghanistan:

"In 1979, after the Soviet invasion of Afghanistan, the CIA and Pakistan's ISI (Inter-Services Intelligence) launched the largest covert operation in the history of the CIA" (Roy).

By foregrounding these historical details, Roy refutes the notion that 9/11 was an isolated act of hatred against "freedom." Instead, she presents it as a tragic consequence of decades of covert operations, funding of militant groups, and political manipulations.

This argument is reinforced by scholarly sources that critique American interventions. Noam Chomsky, for example, similarly argues that *"the U.S. has long supported violent regimes and insurgencies, only to later suffer from the consequences of its policies"* (Chomsky 45). Such a perspective aligns with Roy's assertion that American foreign policy often prioritizes short-term strategic gains over long-term stability.

Roy's dismantling of the phrase "Operation Infinite Justice" is a particularly compelling moment in the essay. She critiques the American military's initial name for its intervention in Afghanistan, pointing out the theological implications:

"It was pointed out that this could be seen as an insult to Muslims, who believe that only Allah can mete out infinite justice, and was renamed Operation Enduring Freedom" (Roy).

Here, Roy exposes the arrogance embedded in American military terminology, where justice is framed as an act of divine retribution rather than a diplomatic or humanitarian endeavor. The rhetorical shift from "infinite justice" to "enduring freedom" does little to conceal the underlying imperial motivations, which Roy astutely identifies.

Scholar Judith Butler echoes this critique of American justifications for war, stating that *"the U.S. narrative of infinite justice functions as a means of deflecting scrutiny from its own geopolitical interests and historical culpabilities"* (Butler 28). This scholarly perspective further validates Roy's argument that American rhetoric often disguises political and military ambitions under the pretence of moral duty.

Another notable rhetorical device Roy employs is juxtaposition, particularly in how she contrasts American grief with the global indifference to non-Western suffering. She writes:

"It must be hard for ordinary Americans, so recently bereaved, to look up at the world with their eyes full of tears and encounter what might appear to them to be indifference. It isn't indifference. It's just augury. An absence of surprise." (Roy).

By positioning American grief alongside the longstanding suffering of civilians in Iraq, Palestine, and Afghanistan, Roy forces the reader to acknowledge a broader spectrum of global violence. This approach is particularly effective in challenging the exceptionalism that often accompanies Western narratives of terrorism.

Scholar Mahmood Mamdani reinforces this point by arguing that *"the U.S. selectively mourns its own losses while erasing the histories of its victims in the Global South"* (Mamdani 67). Such scholarship underscores Roy's critique of America's self-absorbed response to 9/11, which, rather than fostering introspection, led to militarized retribution.

In "The Algebra of Infinite Justice," Arundhati Roy delivers a searing indictment of American foreign policy, exposing its historical amnesia and rhetorical duplicity. Through her sharp irony, historical references, and ethical concerns, she compels the reader to move beyond the dominant Western narrative and consider the broader implications of war. By juxtaposing American grief with global suffering, Roy forces her audience to reckon with uncomfortable truths, making her essay not just a critique of a particular moment in history but a timeless examination of power and justice.

Works Cited

Butler, Judith. Precarious Life: The Powers of Mourning
     and Violence. Verso, 2004.
Chomsky, Noam. Hegemony or Survival: America's Quest
     for Global Dominance. Metropolitan Books, 2003.
Mamdani, Mahmood. Good Muslim, Bad Muslim:
     America, the Cold War, and the Roots of Terror.
     Pantheon Books, 2004.
Roy, Arundhati. "The Algebra of Infinite Justice." The
     Guardian, 29 Sept. 2001,
     www.theguardian.com/world/2001/sep/29/septem
     ber11.usa4.

Vow of Silence: A Feminist Outlook in *That Long Silence* by Shashi Deshpande

Ms. R. G. Sushmaa
Ph.D Scholar, Department of English (Aided),
Kongunadu Arts & Science College (Autonomous), Coimbatore

Dr. R. Sumathi
Assistant Professor, Department of English (Aided),
Kongunadu Arts & Science College (Autonomous), Coimbatore

Dr. P. Sujatha
Assistant Professor, Department of English (Aided),
Kongunadu Arts & Science College (Autonomous), Coimbatore

Silence is a symbolic representation of oppression. One chooses silence over action in terms of submission or surrender in a lost battle. Women had given up faith and hope for a long period of time when they never realised that they had a chance against patriarchal dominance of men in their lives. Evolution happens with a lot of struggles, and feminism was one rebellious act that put an end to the procured trauma and depression that women dealt with all their lives. Feminism is a political movement which originated in the late eighteenth century in Europe. The movement advocates the principle of equality between men and women in terms of rights, education, compensation and much more. The phases of feminism have replaced layers of gender discrimination, chauvinism and female oppression.

Shashi Deshpande is one among the women writers who voiced for feminism. She was a recipient of the 'Sahitya Akademi Award' in 1990 for her fifth novel, *That*

Long Silence in 1988, which was recognized as one among her excellent novels that primarily deals with the problems of women in the present social context, especially in Indian families. Jaya, the protagonist in *That Long Silence*, is often associated with bi-gender identities concerning her personality and behaviour. She is taught to be a woman from the early stages of childhood when she plays joyfully or when she chuckles loudly, by her grandmother. Throughout the novel, several incidents trace out how the societal expectations that are imbued on women, what is expected out of her rather than what she wants. Despite Jaya's success as an intelligent woman with a degree in English, a writer and a columnist, none of these attributes would ever provide her with respectable position in society or in the eyes of her husband, Mohan.

"I was born. My father died when I was fifteen. I got married to Mohan. I have two children and I did not let a third alive" (Deshpande 45). Mohan was build into a dominating household where his father held the upper hand. It is difficult for him to conceive the idea of injustice that was bestowed upon Jaya when he chose to lead a secular life despite being a primary witness to both his mother's and sister's trauma all his life. Their marital life was a constant clockwork, so mechanical that Jaya could never tell any difference between the days of her life. The prosaic existence forces her to question the intimacy of her marriage, the unnecessary need to wait for prosperity only perils as time goes on.

As we grew into young women, we realized it was not love, but marriage that was the destiny waiting for us….and so, with young man, there was the excitement of thinking will this man be my husband? ….It had been our parents who had taken vague desires of ours and translated them into hard facts. It was like the game we had played as children on our buttons tinker, tailor, soldier, sailor…. (Deshpande 19)

Arranged marriages in Indian families pressurize the couple with the fear of responsibility. A woman's dream gets shattered before being formed, claiming it to be a destiny waiting to happen. Jaya, or the other women in the novel, never feared the concept of marriage until they recognize the activities of their partners in the long run. Mohan's father was an abusive drunk, who beat his mother and his children on a regular basis, but the only thing he learnt from this terrible memory was that his mother chose silence and believed that to be the right way.

A woman can never be angry; she can only be neurotic, hysterical, frustrated. There is no room for anger in my life, no room for despair, either. There's only order and routine – today I have to change the sheets; tomorrow, scrub the bathrooms; the day after, clean the fridge . . . (Deshpande 148)

Jaya was not the only victim in her household. Women had taken the vow of silence all around her. Her maternal aunt Vanita Mami, believed that being a devotional could help her bear children even when she got ovarian cancer due to an extreme diet, but she kept having ignorant faith, and no one tried to help her. Mohan's mother died due to abortion as her body could no longer bear the pain of child bearing and this truth was hidden from Mohan by his sister as it was not something that men should be aware of as it might make them awkward. This one incident shows the truth about society and the media, how they visualise menstruation. The process of it is never known to men and thus they never know the pain or suffering of women. Maybe if men were aware of such things, it would build them to stand up for justification of rights for women, but the patriarchal society never lets them to engulf the guilt that they should have encumbered with their actions, thus the dominance continues without any repercussions.

Vimala, Mohan's sister, also dies in a coma by covering the fact that she had ovarian cancer but stays silent without disclosing it to her family as she knows it won't make a difference. Jeeja, Jaya's maid, lets her husband have extra marital affairs as she is manipulated into thinking that she is an undeserving wife as she cannot perform her womanly duties by giving her husband more children even though she is a geriatric woman. Comparatively, Nayana, a help mate of Jaya, is forced by her husband to keep giving birth to children until he has claimed a male child as his next of kin. In one way or another, women had felt oppression in different forms from men but had always chosen silence without any choice.

This man… it had been a revelation to me that two people a man and woman could talk this way. With this man I had not been a woman. I had been just myself — Jaya. There had been ease in our relationship, I had never known in any other. There had been nothing I could not say to him. (Deshpande 153)

Jaya had found companionship with Kamat, her neighbour with whom she could freely express herself, one that could have never been possible with Mohan. Her faith in men was restored when she met Kamat but she still blamed society for cowardice to reacting to the situation they are in. She realised how far she had gone from modernity when she thought twice about helping a sick man to his safety as she withheld untouchability with a friend, made her realise her mistake.

Jaya never knew about Mohan's discrepancies at work until they became homeless. Trust was never the issue in their marriage, but this incident makes Jaya recall her entire life of living a lie through various identities. From being Jaya, the name given at birth by her father to Suhasini, the one given by her husband, along with Seetha, the mythical portrayal of societal expectations of a woman, Jaya, lost her identity. Her marriage to Mohan never let her see the truth of how she was veiled into the object of a woman without her consent. With help from Kamat, Jaya finds her identity and she decides to turn over a new leaf and restore her marriage.

"A sheltering tree. Without the tree you're dangerously unprotected and vulnerable. This... followed logically; and so you have keep the tree alive and flourishing even if you have to water it with deceit and lies" (Deshpande 32). The title of the novel depicts the female psyche of the protagonist Jaya, how she chose the Gandhian principle of life. She chose not to voice out her battles which could turn into dispute by choosing the allusive act of non-violence. She remained silent as she believed that was the womanly way. But one can only hold their breath so long in the water as it isn't practical.

Jaya's mother refers to men in the family as "sheltering tree" as they are the providers of the family and advice Jaya to keep up her marriage even if she has to lie. But in reality, the "sheltering tree", suits Jaya, rather than her husband Mohan, as it was a symbolic representation of the traditional roots of an Indian family with women being the backbone and bearer of all, stuck firmly to their place with no choice. Jaya thought that she should uphold her traditional values by keeping silent but that only destroyed her marriage further. Thus, she decides to actually converse with Mohan, to get her life on track and also to take up responsibility for her share of the marriage by not repeating the same mistakes again.

The feminist writings of Indian literature highlight the pathetic situation of women in the male-dominated society in familial matters or in general. To find peace in life, one should start taking care of one's own home, as harmony at home provides peace of mind and life. A family should practice democracy and the partners in marriage should socialise to get to know each other better so that they can keep up a healthy life. Gender equality is still a struggle in many parts of the world, but everyone should understand and be educated about its outcome and influence on the later generations before exercising it. Feminism is not about berating men, but helping them notice what was wrong and what could have been done to make life better for both men and women.

Works Cited

Deshpande, Shashi. *That Long Silence*. Penguin Books, 1989.

Anu, M. "Awaken of the Suppressed Soul in Shashi Deshpande's That Long Silence." Shanlax International Journal of English 6.S1 (2018): 1-4.

Anuradha, S. "Social marginality in Sashi Deshpande's That long silence." *Conference Editorial Board*. 2015.

Kapoor, Maninder, and Seema Singh. "'[After] That Long Silence: A Feminist Narratological study of Shashi Deshpande." *Journal of Postcolonial Culture and Societies* 3.1948-1842 (2012): 63-90.

Kamu, K., and M. Phil Scholar. "The Quest for Female Identity in Shashi Deshpande's That Long Silence." *Language in India* 19.9 (2019).

An Overview of Arundhati Roy's Novels: A Comprehensive Analysis

Dr. R. Sumathi
Assistant Professor, Department of English (Aided),
Kongunadu Arts & Science College (Autonomous), Coimbatore

Dr. P. Sujatha
Assistant Professor, Department of English (Aided),
Kongunadu Arts & Science College (Autonomous), Coimbatore

Ms. V. M. Anusheya
Ph.D Scholar, Department of English (Aided),
Kongunadu Arts & Science College (Autonomous), Coimbatore

Arundhati Roy stands out as an exceptional writer in the contemporary era, possessing a genuine, rebellious, and reformative voice. Her debut novel, "The God of Small Things," earned her the prestigious Man Booker Prize in 1997. In contrast to many female writers, Roy traverses the less conventional path in her literary works, addressing the harsh realities embedded in society. Unwavering in her commitment to tackling felonious issues, she fearlessly expresses her views through both writing and speaking.

Roy's literary repertoire extends beyond "The God of Small Things" to encompass works such as 'War is Peace' (2001), 'Power Politics' (2001), 'The Greater Common Good' (1999), 'The End of Imagination' (1998), 'The Algebra of Infinite Justice' (2001), 'The Cost of Living' (1999), 'The Shape of the Beast' (2008), 'Kashmir: The Case for Freedom' (2011), 'Capitalism: A Ghost Story' (2014), 'An Ordinary Person's Guide to Empire' (2004), 'War Talk' (2003), and 'The Ministry of Utmost Happiness' (2017). These diverse works delve into political issues, religious concerns, war, capitalism, nationalism, and the plight of people in critical times.

Arundhati Roy is not only renowned for her literary contributions but also for her impactful social activism, actively participating in various revolts aimed at bringing about societal change. Her writing is infused with a purpose; every action seeks to improve the conditions of the underprivileged. A globally acclaimed author and successful social activist, Roy challenges artificial traditions and questions patriarchal ways of life, scrutinizing the authority of political power over people. Her works serve as expressions of her discontent, anger, dissatisfaction, and empathy. She admits-

"I believe writers exist as two entities. One part of me actively lives my life, while the other aspect observes this existence from a detached standpoint — the writer who sits back and watches. This duality doesn't diminish the passion with which I live my life; however, there's always a part of me perched on the ceiling fan, observing with a smile. In all my experiences and endeavors, there's a consistent thread of anger towards authority. The thought of having a child even frightens me because I resist the idea of exerting authority over someone so small. It's a perpetual state of confusion for both myself and those close to me. The questioning of every detail, every sentence, becomes a constant barrier, at times exhausting. These emotions often stem from childhood experiences, and despite growing into adulthood, nothing can suppress these persistent questions, fears, or anger. They persist. Yet, people who know me might describe me as calm. Indeed, in my daily interactions, I exude a sense of calmness. However, this calmness doesn't extend to major issues or profound questions. It's not a loud, shouting anger but rather a cold, simmering one." (Roy, 2017).

Roy actively participated in various protests, including those against the Sardar Sarovar Dam project, which displaced many impoverished families. Her opposition extended to the construction of the Narmada Dam, documented in her essay titled 'The Greater Common Good.' This commitment to highlighting the neglected lives of the marginalized is not new; in 'The God of Small Things,' Roy vividly depicted the internal and external struggles of the Ipe family in the Kerala village of Ayemenem. The novel delves into the intense societal obsession with the class system, untouchability, and the resulting filth that fosters hatred, cruel deaths, and violence. Beyond these societal critiques, the narrative explores the complexities of family and relationships, narrated from Rahel's perspective, seamlessly weaving between childhood and adulthood.

In 'The God of Small Things,' Roy challenges traditional Indian thinking, questioning societal norms and stating, "*They all broke rules. They all crossed into forbidden territory. They all tampered with laws that lay down who should be loved and how. And how much*" (123).

Roy's distinctive style is also evident in "The Ministry of Utmost Happiness," released in 2017 after a prolonged hiatus from fiction writing. The narrative addresses gender discrimination, religious disparities, and political dominance leading to the unjust assassination of innocent individuals. The story centres around Anjum, a transgender individual formerly known as Aftab, born into an orthodox Muslim family. Anjum faces rejection from her father and the fear of societal abandonment. The novel poignantly captures the struggles of Anjum's identity, questioning whether she will find recognition, status, and respect or face societal exclusion.

Growing up, Aftab developed a keen interest in music, but the taunts from fellow students forced him to abandon both his studies and musical pursuits. Concerned parents, desperate for a solution to what they perceived as their child's unconventional identity, took Aftab to a sexologist named Dr. Ghulam Nabi. Contrary to their expectations, Dr. Nabi declared that Aftab was not, medically speaking, a Hijra—a female trapped in a male body (16). Despite this revelation, Aftab found an unexpected happiness, free from the internal strife that plagues many transgender individuals as they grapple with societal acceptance and self-acceptance.

Embracing the identity of Anjum, Aftab sought solace among other transgender individuals living in Khwabgah. Severing ties with his family, Anjum discovered a newfound comfort and acceptance within this community. However, the broader Indian society remains indifferent, if not hostile, towards the transgender community, leading them to beg for survival. Roy vividly captures Anjum's transformation, struggles, and plight, symbolizing the challenges faced by every transgender person in a supposedly democratic country.

The text also sheds light on the darker aspects of multicultural India, where diverse races, castes, religions, and faiths coexist. Yet, societal imbalances often escalate into violence, particularly in the recurring clashes between Muslims and Hindus. Roy addresses the tragic fate of Kashmiri Pandits, who faced massacres, prompting their migration to the plains due to the government's failure to protect them. The narrative also explores the discrimination against Muslim boys, arrested under suspicion of planning terrorist attacks. Anjum, fortunately, escapes harm as the attackers hesitates, considering it a sin to kill a Hijra. This deep-rooted animosity surfaces in mass killings triggered by issues such as cow protection, reflecting the religious tensions within Indian society.

"You had better chased out these old cows that you have here, she said.' If they die here-not if, when they die – they will say you killed them and that will be the end of all of you. They must have their eyes on this property now. That's how they do it these days. They accuse you of eating beef and then take over your house and your land and send you to refugee camp. It's all about property, not cows. You have to be very careful." (402)

Roy adeptly sheds light on contemporary critical and sensitive socio-political issues prevalent in India, revealing the stark realities that persist beneath the façade of secularism and democracy. Her narrative exposes the routine practice of intolerance, racism, discrimination, and injustice, where people are mercilessly slaughtered, and innocents are buried in the shadows. The text serves as an unfiltered truth, unearthing the harsh realities often obscured.

Notably, Roy chooses a transgender protagonist, Anjum, providing readers with a unique perspective on a life typically deemed a curse by society. Anjum's story becomes a window into a world that many overlook, challenging preconceived notions. Unapologetically, Anjum embraces her identity, fearlessly forging the path she desires. She constructs her version of paradise, 'Jannat,' and extends her family by adopting a girl named Zainab.

Beyond highlighting the struggles of the transgender community, Roy confronts the inhuman treatment meted out to the Dalits. These marginalized individuals face systemic barriers that deprive them of opportunities for self-development. Lack of awareness and knowledge condemns them to a life of injustice, perpetuating a cycle of discrimination and neglect.

"In 2008 the situation much worst inside the forest. Operation Green Hunt is announced by Government. War against people. Thousands of police and paramilitary are in the

forest. Killing adivasis, burning villages. No adivasi can stay in her house or their village. They sleep in the forest outside at night because at night police come, hundred, two hundred, sometimes five hundred police. They take everything, burn everything, steal everything. Chickens, goats, money. They want adivasi people to vacate forest so they can make a steel township and mining." (421)

As she described the situation of such underprivileged Dalits, who are forced to leave they own native place and deprived from their civil rights. Roy presented the lives naxals in the forest. They are don't chose to do a hunger strike and request the government for their rights. They chose to lift their arms with guns to snatch their privileges as citizens of democratic country like India. In the letter of Jebeen's real mother, a maoist explains every incident. She left her child because she cannot take care of her. She was raped by police man who are on duty and resulted this child. As she has to live in forest, she gave up the child for her future. This was the reality which never heard or seen. Poor women had to shut her mouth. As it is believed that it's easy to suppress a woman. The scream of women is always remained unheard. They are taught to bear all the pain silently just because they live in a society where all laws are made to control life of women in name of culture and tradition. Another important character of the novels is Tillotama also humiliated and gone through mental torture as she married to a militant named Musa. Arifa and Miss Jebeen also shot to death in the violence in Kashmir. The political interference in Kashmir lead to many deaths and has influenced the peace of the whole country. As the writer pus it Kashmir will make India self-destructive. Roy has been protesting against the government projects which forced people to sacrifice their wellbeing. She has been standing for the rights of women. Through her writing she makes her voice louder. In her interview with John Cusack, she reveals her noble intentions. She says-

"While there is no real opposition to him in the parliament, India's a very interesting place...there is genuine on the ground opposition. If you travel around – there are all kinds of people, brilliant people... journalists, activists, filmmakers, whether you go to Kashmir, the Indian part, or to an Adivasi village about to submerged by a dam reservoir-the level of understanding of everything we have talked about-surveillance, globalization, Ngo-ization- is so high, you know? The wisdom of resistance movements which are ragged and tattered and pushed to the wall, is incredible. So ...look to them and keep the faith" (65).

Roy used the metaphor of a tree to describe the life of Anjum. She describes-

"She lived in the graveyard like a tree. At dawn she saw the crows off and welcomed the bats home. At dusk she did the opposite. Between shifts she conferred with the ghosts of vultures that loomed in her high branches. She felt gentle grip of their talons like an ache in an amputated limb. She gathered they weren't altogether unhappy at having excused themselves and exited from the story" (3).

In the very first paragraph Roy made very clear the protagonist Anjum is an epitome of strength, patience and power. She has the courage to accept the feminine side as well as the nasty opinion of people about her being a transgender. She has the power to transform the graveyard into a heaven for herself and create a new world. As a tree she also opened the doors for other helpless rejected people. Roy completely contradicts the belief of the society that transgender is abnormal. Roy showed concerns for the growing environmental decay due to deforestation, sewage system and mining projects affecting the ecosystem. As per the government's order Adivasi forced to leave their village so that they can build industries and town. It not only affects the inhabitant but also the animals that live in the forest. The Bhopal gas leak incident in India affected the thousand lives. It caused deaths and some of them became permanently blind. *"The Union Carbide pesticide plant in Bhopal sprang a deadly gas leak that killed thousands of people. The newspapers were full of accounts people trying to flee the poisonous cloud that perused them, their eyes and lungs on fire. There was something almost biblical about the nature and the scale of horror."* (151) The poor is exploited in every other way for the benefit of the nation economy. There is a very narrow space for the queers in Indian literature. Sexuality always remains taboo in our conservative society. Those matters never discussed publically so the space for transgender remains inside the walls taboo. Their lives remain a forbidden story. They are neither encouraged to have a better life nor get help from anyone. Some of writers have written on sexuality emphasizing on their place in the society.

Some writers attempted to explore the space, 'The Pregnant King' and 'Shikhandi: And other Tales, They Don't tell you' By Devdutt Pattanaik explains the origin of queers in the mythical texts of ancient ages. Other than that'She of the Mountains' by Vivek Shraya and 'Funny Boy' by Shyam Selvadurai explores the sexuality as well as social and political inferences in the personal interest of the individuals. Arundhati Roy is known for her presentation of unconventional subjects, in this particular work she chooses the unspoken, ignored, underestimated Hijra. India is never a utopia for the trans genders. They are abandoned from the mainstream society. The homophobic society never treated them as complete human beings. They lost their identity and remain silent. Roy exposed the small world of transgender with bigger complications in desperate need of help The Ministry of Utmost Happiness is a complete satire aiming to attack the ways of patriarch society and where a transgender begs for their place, women are raped and bound to seize their lips, abandoned lives of dalits and Hindus and Muslims war. The blind government is taking all of political advantages from those events. The actual victims are the citizens. Roy always captures real events in her texts and this so-called fiction is no less. The story takes us through the lanes between the graveyards to Valley, forest to protest field, and silent tears to demonstration. Apart from a social reformer, Roy is famous for her wonderful use of words. Every word of her work has a purpose. Her remarks about the political situation always attracted controversy because very few writers use the medium of literature to speak the truth. She never thought of popularity or awards or rejections. But she always attempts to sooth the wounds of the excluded crowd. She tries to see through their eyes, aims to console them, help them and stand with them.

References

Barry, Peter. Beginning Theory: An Introduction to
        Literary and Cultural Theory. 3rd Ed, Manchester
        UP,2008.

Roy, Arundhati. The God of small things. Penguin
        Random House India,1997.

---. Things that can and cannot be Said. Juggernaut Books
        India,2016.

 ---.The Ministry of Utmost Happiness. Penguin Random
        House India, 2017. Interview with Arundhati
        Roy./.LastAccessed on 25.3.2018

Posthumanism and the Deconstruction of Identity in Jeet Thayil's poem "Declaration of Intent"

Mr. A. Marappan
Assistant Professor of English
KG College of Arts & Science, Coimbatore

Jeet Thayil's poem "Declaration of Intent" presents a rich imagery and themes that resonate with contemporary societal dynamics. Applying 21st-century literary theories, particularly posthumanism and digital humanities, allows for a nuanced analysis of the poem's exploration of identity, technology, and human experience.

Posthumanism challenges traditional human-centered perspectives, emphasizing the integration of technology and the redefinition of what it means to be human. Thayil's poem encapsulates this by portraying a figure whose existence transcends conventional human limitations. The line, "Your lips go from sunny side to suicide in a single click," juxtaposes warmth with despair, suggesting a rapid shift in states akin to digital interactions. This reflects the posthuman concept of fluid identities in a technologically mediated world. Scholar Cary Wolfe's assertion that posthumanism *"decenters the human in favor of a more inclusive perspective that considers the interaction of biological, technological, and cultural elements"* aligns with this theme in the poem (Wolfe, 2010).

The depiction of "soldiers...of all ages, genders and religious denominations" united solely by the image of the central figure indicates a collective identity formed through shared digital or ideological connections, rather than traditional societal structures. This aligns with posthumanist views on the dissolution of individual boundaries in favor of networked existences. Scholar N. Katherine Hayles, in her exploration of posthumanist themes, suggests that *"the posthuman subject is an amalgam, a collection of heterogeneous components, a material-informational entity"* (Hayles, 1999). Thayil's poem mirrors this idea by presenting a world where individuals are defined not by their physical or cultural boundaries but by their connection to a central, transcendent entity.

The poem's references to technology are evident in lines like, "You invented electricity. The grids belong to you. They blaze your praises, visible from rocket ship and satellite." Here, Thayil acknowledges the pervasive influence of technological advancements and their role in shaping modern identity and perception. The imagery of grids and satellites underscores the omnipresence of digital networks in contemporary life. Scholar JussiParikka notes that *"the spatiality of networks has redefined human interaction, embedding it within the technological environment itself"* (Parikka, 2010). The statement, "Your power is sustainable and biodegradable. Your green will outlast plastic," juxtaposes organic and synthetic elements, highlighting the tension between nature and technology. This reflects digital humanities' interest in how digital culture interacts with environmental concerns and the materiality of technology. Thayil's juxtaposition suggests an aspiration for harmony between human innovation and ecological sustainability.

Thayil's work often incorporates intertextual elements, drawing from various cultural and literary sources. The poem's structure and thematic concerns may echo traditional poetic forms while embedding contemporary issues, creating a dialogue between the past and present. Scholar Linda Hutcheon's theory of historiographic metafiction emphasizes the use of intertextuality as a means to critique historical and cultural narratives (Hutcheon, 1988). In "Declaration of Intent," Thayil invokes this approach by crafting a poem that feels timeless yet distinctly modern, engaging with global anxieties about identity and technology.

Despite its technological imagery, the poem delves deeply into human emotions. Lines such as, *"Your tears are the end of seasons,"* and, *"If you speak to yourself your unheard words will make a stranger stop in grief,"* evoke profound emotional responses, suggesting that, even in a posthuman context, fundamental human experiences like sorrow and empathy persist. Scholar Martha Nussbaum posits that literature's engagement with emotions fosters an understanding of ethical dilemmas and shared humanity (Nussbaum, 1995). Thayil's poetic exploration reflects this idea, intertwining technology and emotion to question the essence of human connection.

The poem also critiques the fleeting and performative aspects of modern existence. The line *"Your lips go from sunny side to suicide in a single click"* underscores the ephemerality of digital interactions and their emotional consequences. Scholar Sherry Turkle's work on the psychology of online behavior emphasizes that *"the constant connectivity of the digital world reshapes the way we experience intimacy and identity"* (Turkle, 2011). Thayil captures this dynamic, portraying a world where emotional states are as transient as digital communications.

"Declaration of Intent" serves as a compelling exploration of identity in the digital age, reflecting posthumanist themes and the pervasive influence of technology on human experience. Thayil's integration of vivid imagery and emotional depth invites readers to contemplate the evolving nature of selfhood and connection in a rapidly changing world. The poem's dual focus on technological advancement and enduring human emotion aligns with the broader discourse in contemporary literature, where the boundaries between the organic and the digital blur, giving rise to new forms of identity and understanding.

The poem's tension between individuality and collectivism is particularly poignant in the context of globalized networks. As Thayil writes, *"They blaze your praises, visible from rocket ship and satellite,"* he reflects on the performative aspects of identity in the digital age, where visibility often equates to validation. Scholar Manuel Castells describes this phenomenon as *"the shift from being to appearing, mediated by the pervasive influence of the network society"* (Castells, 2000). This interplay between authenticity and spectacle underscores the fragility of contemporary selfhood.

The poem addresses the environmental implications of technological progress. The juxtaposition of "your power is sustainable and biodegradable" with "your green will outlast plastic" illustrates the paradox of technological innovation: its capacity for both preservation and destruction. Digital humanities scholars have increasingly focused on the ecological footprint of technology, emphasizing the need for sustainable practices in an increasingly digitized world. Scholar Richard Maxwell suggests that *"the digital economy is deeply entwined with material and environmental consequences, necessitating a reevaluation of its impact"* (Maxwell, 2015). Thayil's poem implicitly critiques the consumerist underpinnings of technological innovation while envisioning a more harmonious coexistence.

In conclusion, Jeet Thayil's "Declaration of Intent" is a multifaceted exploration of identity, technology, and human experience through the lens of posthumanism and digital humanities. By intertwining vivid imagery with profound emotional depth, Thayil crafts a poetic narrative that resonates with contemporary societal concerns. The poem challenges readers to rethink the essence of selfhood, the implications of technological progress, and the enduring significance of human emotions. Through its rich tapestry of themes and imagery, "Declaration of Intent" stands as a testament to the power of poetry to engage with and illuminate the complexities of the modern world.

Works Cited

Castells, Manuel. *The Rise of the Network Society*. Wiley-Blackwell, 2000.

Hayles, N. Katherine. *How We Became Posthuman: Virtual Bodies in Cybernetics, Literature, and Informatics*. University of Chicago Press, 1999.

Hutcheon, Linda. *A Poetics of Postmodernism: History, Theory, Fiction*. Routledge, 1988.

Maxwell, Richard. *Greening the Media*. Oxford University Press, 2015.

Nussbaum, Martha. *Poetic Justice: The Literary Imagination and Public Life*. Beacon Press, 1995.

Parikka, Jussi. *Media Ecologies: Materialist Energies in Art and Technoculture*. MIT Press, 2010.

Thayil, Jeet. "Declaration of Intent." *Poetry International*, 2015.

Turkle, Sherry. *Alone Together: Why We Expect More from Technology and Less from Each Other*. Basic Books, 2011.

Wolfe, Cary. *What Is Posthumanism?* University of Minnesota Press, 2010.

Exploring Trauma in Adil Jussawalla's "Silhouette": A Critical Analysis

Mr S. Shanthosh Kumar

Assistant Professor of English
VLB Janakiammal College of Arts & Science, Coimbatore

Adil Jussawalla's Silhouette is a poignant exploration of the lingering effects of political violence and psychological scars left by historical events. The poem, set against the backdrop of post-Emergency India, uses fragmented imagery and evocative language to portray trauma—both personal and collective. Applying the frameworks of Cathy Caruth, Dominick LaCapra, and Judith Herman from trauma studies offers valuable insights into the themes of memory, repression, and healing in the poem.

Cathy Caruth, in her seminal work Unclaimed Experience: Trauma, Narrative, and History (1996), argues that trauma is not fully graspable at the moment of its occurrence. Instead, it is relived repeatedly through involuntary memories and narratives. Caruth writes, *"The impact of the traumatic event lies precisely in its belatedness, in its refusal to be simply located"* (Caruth 8).

In Silhouette, this belatedness is evident in the imagery of the broken figure whose trauma resists resolution. The poem describes a silhouette that *"hits out and runs, hits nothing, runs."* This haunting depiction captures the futile, repetitive actions of someone trapped in the cycle of their trauma. Twenty years later, the silhouette's feet are "broken," and it remains unable to move forward. The line "Will it lie on a plank for days, twisting a handkerchief?" reflects the psychological paralysis and obsessive reliving of the event.

Caruth's emphasis on the connection between trauma and narrative helps explain why the speaker wishes the silhouette "a straighter back, a stronger earth." These wishes signify a desire for the figure to escape its repetitive suffering, though the inability to move on underscores the unresolved nature of its trauma.

Dominick LaCapra, in Writing History, Writing Trauma (2001), distinguishes between "acting out" and "working through" trauma. "Acting out" refers to compulsive repetition of traumatic experiences, while "working through" involves a more critical engagement that allows for partial healing. LaCapra also emphasizes the importance of contextualizing trauma within historical and political frameworks, noting that *"Historical trauma…is bound up with the specificities of the past and the historical forces involved"* (LaCapra 77).

In Silhouette, the historical context of the Emergency (1975–1977) looms large. The lines "Emergency means Discipline" and "A man with a face as flat as a hand" invoke the authoritarian suppression of dissent during that period. These references ground the poem's portrayal of trauma in a specific socio-political moment. The silhouette, representing the silenced victims of state violence, embodies the "acting out" of historical trauma—unable to move beyond its brokenness.

The speaker's reflection on the silhouette, however, hints at a desire for "working through." The acknowledgment of its pain ("It has my best wishes") and the hope for a stronger future suggest an effort to reconcile with the past. Nevertheless, the speaker's detachment ("Ravi studies his car keys and is silent") underscores the challenge of engaging deeply with collective suffering, illustrating LaCapra's observation that "working through trauma is both necessary and incomplete" (LaCapra 90).

Judith Herman's Trauma and Recovery (1992) explores the long-term psychological effects of trauma, emphasizing its disruption of memory, identity, and relationships. Herman argues that *"trauma obliterates the sense of self...and ruptures the bond between the individual and community"* (Herman 51). Her work is particularly relevant in understanding the personal dimension of trauma in Silhouette.

The silhouette's fragmented identity is evident in its portrayal as an abstract, broken figure. The poem's focus on physical and emotional disintegration ("Will its hands fly to its face when a light's switched on?") aligns with Herman's assertion that trauma victims often experience hyperarousal and emotional dysregulation. The image of the silhouette "twisting a handkerchief" conveys an obsessive, repetitive coping mechanism that underscores the persistence of its psychological wounds.

Herman also highlights the importance of community in trauma recovery, noting that *"the restoration of social bonds...is the core of recovery"* (Herman 61). In the poem, however, this restoration remains elusive. Ravi's silence and the noise of "clouds, not far, [making] a noise like MiGs" reflect an environment where communal healing is overshadowed by lingering fears and memories of violence.

The three trauma theorists converge in illuminating the multi-layered portrayal of trauma in Silhouette. Caruth's concept of repetition explains the silhouette's cyclical suffering and inability to escape the past. LaCapra's distinction between acting out and working through sheds light on the poem's oscillation between acknowledgment and detachment. Meanwhile, Herman's focus on identity and community emphasizes the psychological toll of trauma and the absence of meaningful recovery.

The speaker's ambivalence towards the silhouette captures the tension between these perspectives. On one hand, the wishes for a "straighter back" and "stronger earth" suggest a longing for healing. On the other hand, the speaker's detached tone and Ravi's silence reflect the societal indifference that perpetuates trauma. This ambivalence resonates with Caruth's assertion that trauma is characterized by "a struggle to comprehend and to represent experiences that defy comprehension" (Caruth 5).

Adil Jussawalla's Silhouette is a rich text that intricately explores the enduring effects of trauma. Through the frameworks of Caruth, LaCapra, and Herman, the poem's fragmented narrative and haunting imagery are revealed as profound representations of the psychological, historical, and social dimensions of trauma. By situating the silhouette within both personal and collective contexts, Jussawalla highlights the complexities of memory and recovery, reminding us of the ongoing struggle to make sense of the unspeakable.

Works Cited

Caruth, Cathy. *Unclaimed Experience: Trauma, Narrative, and History*. Johns Hopkins University Press, 1996.

Herman, Judith. *Trauma and Recovery: The Aftermath of Violence – From Domestic Abuse to Political Terror*. Basic Books, 1992.

LaCapra, Dominick. *Writing History, Writing Trauma*. Johns Hopkins University Press, 2001.

Jussawalla, Adil. "Silhouette". 15 March 2018.